FRANK WERNER

The

Amazing Journey

of Adam Smith

To my children and grandchildren

who deserve a better world than

the one we are currently leaving to them.

— *Preface* —

I have been a professor of finance for more than thirty years. At the beginning of my academic career, like most newly minted Ph.D.s, I devoted my energy to understanding the existing theory and literature—how I could advance it with my research, and how I could better explain it to my students with my teaching. I used the same textbooks and taught the same concepts that other finance professors taught. I believed in the veracity and usefulness of what I had learned. Finance was the core business discipline, the one that ensured that businesses succeeded, created jobs, and provided an extensive variety of goods and services to enrich people's lives. Get the finance right and everything else falls into place.

I still believe in the beauty of finance and its power to improve lives. However, somewhere along the way I began to doubt one of its most basic premises: that the goal of the for-profit corporation was to maximize the wealth of its owners.

What bothered me initially were the side effects: fraudulent accounting to convince the stock market a company was worth more than it actually was, child labor to keep costs low and profits high, exorbitant executive pay and perks that exacerbated income disparities. But like many of us who had attended business school, I agreed with the standard argument that these side effects were unavoidable by-products of business efficiency. To the extent the public found them unacceptable, people would use the political process to have their representatives in government pass laws to constrain or prevent them. Like others, I complained about the power of business lobbies, but their presence did not change my view that the goal of finance was still correct.

Over the past decade I have slowly changed my mind. The growing importance of natural capital and human capital made me question the primacy of financial capital as a business resource. The emergence of social construction theory and behavioral finance led me to question the efficiency of financial markets and the rationality of market participants, both necessary for financial market prices to accurately measure and guide managerial behavior. Research on exceptionally successful companies concluded that most did not primarily pursue a financial goal or pursued multiple goals.

The tipping point was global warming. Unlike the other side effects of business efficiency, this one had the potential to cause irreparable damage to the world and possibly even eliminate humans from the Earth. But it was business as usual in the financial community. Maximizing shareholder wealth was still the objective. It simply didn't matter how much fossil fuel we burned or how much rain forest we cut down in the pursuit of profits. It was irrelevant that damaging weather events were becoming more numerous or that serious diseases previously thought to be eradicated were making a reappearance. Finance simply wasn't interested. Of equal concern, government didn't seem to be interested either, or at least interested enough. The laws and regulations that were enacted seemed feeble compared to the relentless march of climate change.

I had seen this phenomenon before, in the 1980s and 1990s, when my colleague and dear friend Jim Stoner and I started asking questions about how the quality management movement was changing finance. When we began that work, many of the finance executives we spoke to had little or no knowledge of quality management. Of those that did, most considered it to apply only to the factory floor. The concepts that finance had customers and processes, and that exceeding the expectations of those customers and improving those processes could add to the bottom line, didn't reach the office of many CFOs until much later. Of course, then the stakes were lower, merely global competitiveness versus global survival today.

I have wanted to tell this story for a while now, to share my disquiet with the finance goal of shareholder wealth maximization. The inspiration to tell it in this way came from my students in the MBA seminars on Finance and Global Sustainability that Jim Stoner and I taught at Fordham University in the Spring and Summer 2008 terms. Thank you, Jim. Thank you, seminar participants. It's wonderful when the professor learns as much as and maybe more than his students.

Further thank yous go to my colleagues, friends, and family members who reviewed drafts of the manuscript and gave me encouraging and helpful comments and insights: Professors John Hollwitz, Dawn Lerman, Michael Pirson, Barbara Porco, and Jim Stoner, and my graduate student assistants Dominique Blanc, Landis Carey, Kim Cariello, and Amanda Trokan at Fordham; Pace University Professors Ghassan Karam and Joe Ryan; Professors William Ferris of Western New England College, Joel Harmon of Fairleigh Dickinson University, and Cheryl Tromley of Fairfield University who joined Jim Stoner and me to discuss the manuscript at a session of the Eastern Academy of Management 2009 annual meeting; friends Jennifer Dolan, Barbara Stevens, and Rob Waldman; cousins and booksellers Betty and John Bennett; my children Allison Werner-

Lin and Eric Werner and their spouses Bill Lin and Sarah Werner; and, most importantly, my wife Marie.

Finally, thank you Adam Smith. I first met you in an economics course in my undergraduate years, and you have remained an inspiration until this day. I couldn't have written this book without you.

The Invisible Hand

Adam Smith put down his pen and reread the words he had just written. The ink was not yet dry, but the letters were clear, written in a bold hand:

> As every individual, therefore, endeavours as much as he can both to employ his capital in the support of domestic industry, and so to direct that industry that its produce may be of the greatest value; every individual necessarily labours to render the annual value of society as great as he can. He generally, indeed, neither intends to promote the public interest, nor knows how much he is promoting it. By preferring the support of domestic to that of foreign industry he intends only his own security; and by directing that industry in such a manner as its produce may be of the greatest value, he intends only his own gain, and he is in

this, as in many other cases, led by an invisible hand to promote an end which was no part of his intention. Nor is it always the worse for the society that it was no part of it. By pursuing his own interest he frequently promotes that of society more effectually than when he really intends to promote it.

It had taken Smith several months to reach this conclusion. For the most part, individuals acted in their own self-interest, a point Smith had made earlier in the new book he was writing, *An Inquiry Into the Nature and Causes of the Wealth of Nations*:

> **It is not from the benevolence of the butcher, the brewer, or the baker, that we expect our dinner, but from their regard to their own interest.**

While others had argued that this would be bad for society at large, Smith saw just the opposite. To make as much money as possible, businessmen would have to respond to the needs of society. Products in short supply would rise in price, increasing profit margins, and more would be produced as businessmen saw the opportunity to make more money. On the other hand, if too much of a product were brought to market, the price would drop and the least profitable producers would cease production and turn to producing other, more profitable goods. The result: supply would match the demand of society and only the most efficient producers of each product would survive.

Smith particularly liked the phrase 'invisible hand.' It was a phrase he had used before, both in his much earlier essay, 'The History of Astronomy' and, more recently, in his well received treatise, *The Theory of Moral Sentiments*:

> ... in spite of their natural selfishness and rapacity, though they mean only their own con-veniency, though the sole end which they propose from the labours of all the thousands whom they employ, be the gratification of their own vain and insatiable desires, they divide with the poor the produce of all their improvements. They are led by an invisible hand to make nearly the same distribution of the necessaries of life, which would have been made, had the earth been divided into equal portions among all its inhabitants, and thus without intending it, without knowing it, advance the interest of the society.

Smith was proud of and excited by his conclusions. There was no disconnect between individual selfishness and greed and the needs of society. The natural forces of the free market would align the two. Industrial output would respond to society's demands. Prices would reach a 'natural level' that would balance supply and demand for every product. Producers would become efficient so that the limited resources of the day would be used wisely

Smith stood up from his desk and walked over to the large window on the other side of his study. He had been writing continuously for several hours, and the sun was well into the western sky. A bright glow fell over the lawn of his Kirkcaldy, Scotland home. He stretched his arms above his head and yawned. It was time for a cup of tea. Smith crossed the room back toward his desk and opened the door to the parlour.

—— A Lecture Hall ——

Adam Smith looked up as he walked through the door and stopped in his tracks. This was not his parlour. He was in the back of a large auditorium, much like one of the halls he had lectured in when he was a professor and occupied the Chair of Moral Philosophy at the University of Glasgow some years ago. But the auditorium was not one that he recognized. In fact, much about the room was very strange.

For one thing, the floor was sloped down from the back of the room toward the front. Smith had rarely seen an auditorium with a floor that was not flat by design. For another, the seats were fixed to the floor and were upholstered—not the stiff-backed, moveable wooden chairs that his students had to sit in. The seats were closer together and there were many more than he was accustomed to. Most strange, the front wall of the auditorium was painted with a picture, a picture that changed every few minutes. He had never before seen a painting with the ability to change, and he was fascinated by it.

The auditorium was filled with people. Smith tried counting them, but it was somewhat dark in the room, and he couldn't be sure that he saw everyone. He made a quick guess that there must have been 400 to 500 people in the hall. To a person, they were staring at the painting on the front wall.

A man was standing on the platform in the front of the auditorium giving a lecture. Smith had never seen him before, but he was clearly comfortable speaking to such a large group. He was speaking English, but not with a Scottish accent, and some of his words and phrases were nothing Smith had ever heard before. 'Probably from the south coast of England,' Smith thought, recalling that people from Cornwall had what to his ear was a quite different accent.

The audience was paying rapt attention to the speaker. Was he a reverend? A professor? He was not wearing the robes common to the clergy and to academe. Rather, he was dressed in a strange sort of suit. His dark blue jacket matched his pants but was far too plain to be in fashion. His shirt was also plain, and it was blue, not white, and had no ruffles around the collar. His cravat was a simple one with alternating red and blue stripes, and it was tied to lay flat against his shirt rather than billow out at the neck. How odd!

Smith turned his attention to the painting on the front wall. It was filled with words and looked like a piece of notepaper. He couldn't imagine what painter would produce such a strange work of art. He began to read the words of the painting, but before he could finish, the painting changed and new words were on the front wall. This time the painting contained a diagram in addition to the words. What was going on?

Smith turned to the woman sitting to his right and asked who the speaker was and what was the topic of the presentation, but she ignored him. He asked the same of the man on his left, and once again he got no response. It was as if he weren't there.

The painting changed once again. With a sigh, Smith settled into his seat and tried to concentrate on what the speaker was saying. Who was he? And what was the meaning of the words of the painting?

First Edition?

Jennifer parked her car on the side of the road, pressed the button on the key fob to lock the doors, and crossed the street to the lawn on the other side. It was the last Saturday in August, the day of the monthly flea market. She was one of the regulars who stopped by every month, warm or cold, rain or shine. Jennifer looked forward to browsing the tables and to socializing with the vendors, many of whom she knew well by now.

She considered herself a person of simple tastes, 'low maintenance' as she liked to joke with Andrew, her fiancé, and the market seemed just the place to shop for clothing and jewelry. The styles were simple and fun, more interesting than at the big-box stores, and the prices sure beat those at the boutiques in the city. The people were nice too, friendly and always helpful.

In addition to her usual shopping, today Jennifer had another mission. Andrew had just been admitted to the MBA program at a local university, and Jennifer wanted to buy him a present to celebrate the event. But what to get? Certainly not clothes or jewelry! She walked toward a group of tables she normally didn't find interesting. Andrew wasn't a car buff, so she passed by the tables with automobile parts and accessories. Neither was he much of a cook, so kitchen tools and appliances were not appropriate either. What else was there?

As she looked around, she spotted a book vendor. Funny that she hadn't noticed this seller before. Perhaps he wasn't a regular seller, or perhaps it was the location, at the far end of the lawn. She walked over to the table and started a conversation with the vendor who was rearranging several of the books. She told him what she was looking for, and he directed her to the only stack of business books he had. He apologized that he didn't have any recommendations for her as business books weren't his specialty, but he encouraged her to check them out nonetheless.

Most of the books didn't seem to be appropriate for what she had in mind. There were government reports on the economy from ten years ago. There were quite a few old textbooks—Jennifer was sure that Andrew would be using newer editions in his studies. There were other books that appeared to be written for a popular audience, but nothing that looked like something Andrew would be particularly interested in.

She was about to give up when she saw a leather-bound book toward the back of the table. 'That's odd,' she thought, since she had looked there less than a minute ago and didn't remember seeing it. Nevertheless, she picked it up. The book's title was *An Inquiry Into the Nature and Causes of the Wealth of Nations.* The author was someone named Adam Smith, and Jennifer had a vague memory that she had heard that name when she took her one economics course in college. Maybe this would be an appropriate gift.

The book appeared to be quite old. Jennifer turned to the copyright page to see when it had been written. The date was 1776. She scanned down the page to see when this edition had been published, but she could not find any other date. She flipped through the first few pages, but 1776 was the only date she found. This couldn't be a first edition, could it? It seemed unlikely since the book was on a table at a country flea market selling for such a low price. On the other hand, if it were a first edition, she had just found something very valuable, and the book would be an amazing gift for Andrew. Jennifer was afraid to ask, just in case it was a rare copy and the price would go way up. She did her best to remain as casual as she could as she paid for the book.

Back at her apartment later in the day, Jennifer carefully wrapped the book using the box and gift paper she had purchased on her way home. She put the book in the top drawer of her dresser and sat down to plan a romantic dinner to celebrate Andrew's achievement.

–4–

Truth

Adam Smith resumed paying attention to the lecture. A painting that the lecturer identified as the earth was on the front wall. The image was indeed that of a sphere, as Smith knew the earth to be, but how was it possible for anyone to paint a picture of what the earth looked like from such a distance? It was as if the painter had set up his easel on the back of one of those turtles that the ancients believed held up the universe!

The lecturer commented on how beautiful the earth looked, and the audience murmured in agreement. He then proceeded to talk about the earth's atmosphere— how relatively thin and fragile it was. A new painting appeared with a diagram showing how the atmosphere captured heat from the sun. The lecturer explained that the atmosphere was getting thicker because it was being polluted by increasing amounts of carbon dioxide (whatever that was!). A painting of a factory spewing dark brown and black gasses into a vivid yellow-orange sky appeared, presumably to emphasize the point, and it was followed on the front wall by a line showing the increasing carbon dioxide levels. A thicker atmosphere, the lecturer continued, was capturing more and more heat from the sun, and that was a big concern. The lecturer called the problem 'global warming.'

Smith wasn't quite sure why having warmth from the sun could be a problem. After all, didn't every living thing on the earth depend on sunlight to survive? Without the sun, there would be no day and night. Plants would not grow. There would be no light by which to see nature's beauty. He continued watching and listening, but with a great degree of skepticism.

The painting changed again, this time to an ice-covered mountain, and just as quickly it changed to another painting of the same mountain without much ice covering at all. Other similar paintings followed in pairs, the first showing a dense ice cover on the ground and the second, the ground nearly bare. The lecturer remarked that the paintings were of glaciers and showed how the increasing atmospheric heat was melting the ice caps at both the north and south poles. 'More water for all to drink,' thought Smith, but that thought quickly evaporated when the lecturer continued. "Forty percent of the world's population gets its drinking water from rivers and streams that themselves get more than half their water from glacial melt. As the glaciers disappear, these people will face a very severe water shortage."

A woman raised her hand, and the lecturer acknowledged her. "Mr. Gore," she asked. "Where will the water from the melting glaciers go? It would have to go somewhere, wouldn't it?"

"Yes it would," Al Gore replied. "The water would flow into the world's oceans, and sea levels would rise. Scientists estimate that if either the West Antarctic ice shelf or Greenland's ice cover were to melt fully—and they're both melting already—the level of the world's oceans would increase by as much as twenty feet. Think about the implications. Historically, people chose where to live based on the climate, the fertility of the land, the availability of water to drink and animals for food, and access to rivers and oceans for transportation. These factors have been pretty much unchanged since the last ice age 11,000 years ago. As a result, most of the world's large cities are located along rivers and coastlines. These computer images show what would happen to some major populated areas if the oceans rose by twenty feet." More paintings appeared on the front wall, and each painting changed as the coastline moved inland to swallow up a part of the land. Smith didn't understand what a 'computer image' was or how Gore accomplished this visual magic, but he was certainly impressed.

Gore continued. "The rising oceans would displace more than 100 million people. The problem of refugees is bad enough today, so imagine if the world had to cope with that degree of upheaval."

"The warming oceans pose other problems. Today we have more intense storms, more hurricanes, more tornados, more typhoons than ever before. People worldwide face the destruction of their homes and cities by the weather to a degree never before experienced in human history." Paintings of a flooded city appeared. Gore identified the city as New Orleans and the destruction as the result of a hurricane named Katrina. Another sequence of paintings showed how the hurricane had intensified before reaching land by passing over a body of water that was warmer than its historical temperature. Smith knew of the city of Orléans south of Paris in France but not New Orleans; nevertheless, he could see that the amount of damage caused by the hurricane was immense.

Gore talked about other effects of global warming. Species of insects, birds, and fish were becoming extinct at rates a thousand times that of the historical average because the temperature of their natural habitats was changing, reducing their food supplies, and this was disrupting the food chain of all species including humans. Serious diseases were spreading as disease-carrying insects were moving into areas that had previously been too cold to support them.

Bit by bit, Smith began to understand the speaker's message. The earth's temperature was rising at an increasing and alarming rate, and this was causing major damage to the world. The cause of the change was something called atmospheric pollution. If the change were to continue, the consequences for the earth would be catastrophic. But how could such a disaster happen? When was it happening? And most important, what was being done to prevent it from getting worse?

5

Back in School

Andrew took a seat in the front-center of the lecture hall. As an undergraduate he typically sat in the back of his classrooms. It was easier to whisper to his friends back there or hide from the professor when he had not prepared the daily assignment. But he was older now. He really wanted to learn as much as he could in his MBA program. By sitting in the front row he would immerse himself totally in the class.

It was the first day of the fall semester, and Andrew was very excited to finally be back in school again. All summer long he had talked about what going back to school meant to him. He was sure Jennifer was tired of hearing him bring the subject up again and again, although she always smiled and seemed interested. It was one of the many things he loved about her.

Five minutes before the hour, a middle-aged man walked in and strode to the front of the hall. He took some papers out of his briefcase and spread them out on the professor's desk. Then he turned to the whiteboard and wrote his name and the name of the course: 'Financial Management.' Andrew considered himself fortunate to be able to start his program with this course. Most MBA students at his school had to wait until the second semester to take their first finance course since accounting and statistics were prerequisites. However, Andrew had taken comparable courses in his undergraduate program and had received high marks in both, so he did not have to repeat them. The students quieted down, and all eyes turned to the front of the room.

"Good afternoon," the professor began. "Today we begin your study of finance. This will be the most important course you will take in your MBA program since finance is at the very core of all businesses. All business decisions have a financial implication, so all decisions must be analyzed through the lens of finance. In fact, the very goal of the business firm is a financial goal: to maximize the wealth of the shareholders."

The professor spent the next twenty minutes going over the requirements of the course: the textbook, topics to be covered, homework assignments, papers, exams, and so on. Then he returned to the subject of the goal of the firm.

"The owners of every for-profit firm are its shareholders. Our legal system has accepted that they are the firm's owners because they bear the ultimate risk of the firm's performance. They have no contract that guarantees them a rate of return. In fact, they have no guarantees at all. If the company does well, they do well. If it does poorly, so do they. And if the firm goes out of business, they typically lose all the money they have invested. In return for taking this risk, the shareholders have the final say about how the firm operates."

"Now, shareholders invest their money in a company for one reason and one reason only: to earn a decent rate of return. Remember, they can always invest their money elsewhere. To use the term you learned in your economics course, if they choose not to invest in another company they bear an 'opportunity cost'—the rate of return they forego. So, every company must provide a competitive rate of return. Now, just what is a competitive rate of return? Well, we'll talk much more about that as the term goes on, but, bottom line, it's a rate of return that is consistent with the general level of interest rates in the economy and also is appropriate for the amount of risk the shareholders are taking by investing in the company."

"So, if the firm does well financially, the shareholders do well." The professor looked up from his notes and looked at the class. "Tell me, how can a firm do well?" he asked.

A student in the back row was the first to raise his hand. "It could make excellent products that people really want," he offered.

"Good," said the professor as Andrew thought 'so much for the people in the back row not paying attention!' "What else?" the professor asked.

Another student raised his hand. "It could be really efficient so it keeps its costs down. That should result in higher profits."

"Agreed," the professor replied. "Anyone else?"

"It could provide excellent customer service," said a woman on the side of the classroom by the windows.

The interchange continued along these lines for about another five minutes. Then the professor summarized the discussion. "So, what we've said is that a firm that makes excellent products and provides top-notch services, makes them at a low cost that enables it to sell them at a competitive price, and satisfies its customers will make high profits. Now, profits don't always translate to immediate value for shareholders—more on this in our next class—but, in general, a company that is highly profitable is one that generates high returns for shareholders. When shareholders find a company that they believe will generate a high rate of return on their investment, they will compete to own the firm's stock, and this will drive the price of the stock up. And since the wealth a company can provide its shareholders is the value of their stock, shareholder wealth will have been increased. This is why the goal of every for-profit company has to be to maximize the wealth of the shareholders—it's identical to giving shareholders the highest possible rate of return on their investment."

The professor looked up at the clock hanging on the wall opposite the windows. Seeing that the class period was coming to an end, he assigned some reading in the textbook and dismissed the class. The students stood up and began chatting about the material and the professor as they made their way out of the room.

Andrew was elated. This was just what he had been hoping for. The professor was clear and had captured his attention, and the subject matter was fascinating. It was great to be back in school!

6

—— *Inconvenient* ——

The picture on the front wall changed once again. This time it was of a graph. The horizontal axis was labeled with numbers beginning with 1000 and continuing to 2000, and Al Gore referred to the scale as years. Could it now be the year 2000? Adam Smith was dumbfounded. If that were accurate, it was now more than 200 years into the future. Could he really be attending an event taking place at the start of the third millennium?

Smith recalled a curious remark the speaker had made toward the beginning of the lecture, that he "used to be the next President of the United States of America." Could that be where he was, in the United States of America? Smith knew that 'United States of America' was a name that had been proposed by some revolutionaries in England's American colonies for the country they were fighting to create. Could it be that England had lost the war? A painful question passed fleetingly through Smith's mind: did England still exist as a country? Maybe it was now part of those new United States!

"This graph shows the average temperature in the northern hemisphere for the past 1,000 years," Gore was saying. He commented on the graph, emphasizing the fluctuations in the world's historical temperature, particularly during the several ice ages. "Nevertheless," he added, pointing to the right-hand side of the graph where the temperature line sloped up sharply, "there is simply no comparison to what is going on now." Gore pressed a button on the box in his hand and a second graph, showing atmospheric carbon dioxide concentrations, appeared to the right of the first. The two graphs were nearly identical!

Gore continued. "Using data from ice layers in Antarctica, we can actually trace carbon dioxide and temperature levels as far back as 650,000 years ago." Smith's mind reeled at the thought of how much science must have advanced since his day for someone to have been able to do that. A new graph showing atmospheric carbon dioxide levels for the past 650 millennia appeared on the front wall. "Notice that in all that time, even with multiple ice ages, the level of carbon dioxide in the atmosphere never exceeded 300 parts per million." Gore pressed the button again, and a second line, representing the earth's temperature over the same period, appeared below the first. Once again the two lines were nearly identical. "While the relationship between atmospheric carbon dioxide and global temperature is a complex one, what is clear is that when there is more carbon dioxide, the earth's temperature gets warmer because the carbon dioxide traps more heat from the sun."

A young man sitting in the front of the auditorium raised his hand. "Sir, where is all this carbon dioxide coming from, and why the huge recent increase?"

"There are two primary sources," Gore responded. "One is the burning of fossil fuels: coal, gas, and petroleum—both directly and to generate electricity—to heat and light our homes, power our factories, and fuel our automobiles and airplanes. The other is deforestation which is typically accomplished by burning and which is going on worldwide at an unprecedented rate. The combustion itself releases carbon dioxide, and then there are fewer trees left to absorb carbon dioxide from the air and emit oxygen. Both have increased significantly in the last few decades as the earth's population has grown and the world has become increasingly industrialized."

Now Gore climbed onto some kind of mechanical platform and rose, as if by magic, into the air. As he did so, the graph extended to the right and the carbon dioxide line rose with him to a level nearly twice as high as the rest of the graph. "Here is where the level of carbon dioxide in the atmosphere is now, far above the natural cycle. And in less than fifty years, here's what it's going to be if there is no change in the way we live." Gore rose still further on his magic platform, and as he did, the carbon dioxide line rose with him, now to a height over three times the historical level. "Imagine what that would mean for the world's temperature. Ultimately, this is really not a political issue so much as a moral issue. If we allow that to happen it is deeply unethical!"

Smith squinted at the picture to make sure he was reading the dates correctly. According to the graph, global warming had become a serious issue in the latter part of the twentieth century, and it was now some 30 to 40 years later. Surely that would have given the governments of the world time to address the problem. Surely such an impending disaster would be the number one topic of every responsible government and every diplomatic discussion. Surely the countries most responsible for global warming would be taking the lead in reversing it.

But Gore's message was quite the opposite. "The United States produces the greatest amount of atmospheric carbon dioxide, yet when I look to our government for a meaningful response, I don't see it. There are good people in politics, in both parties, who hold this at arm's length because if they acknowledge it and recognize it, then the moral imperative to make changes is inescapable."

He continued. "Global warming is an easy issue for many politicians to ignore. For one thing, it's not seen as a 'bread and butter' issue by the average person. For another, the executives of many large corporations fear that addressing the problem would mean they would have to change their business practices in ways that would reduce their profitability. These companies often use their political influence and campaign contributions to encourage politicians to avoid or ignore the issue." He quoted someone named Upton Sinclair: "'It is difficult to get a man to understand something when his salary depends on his not understanding it.' Many laws are influenced or even written by lobbyists specifically to benefit their corporate clients."

Adam Smith smiled. He had made much the same point in *The Wealth of Nations*:

> The proposal of any new law or regulation of commerce which comes from [businessmen] ought always to be listened to with great precaution, and ought never to be adopted, till after having been long and carefully examined, not only with the most scrupulous, but with the most suspicious attention.

Gore went on. "In fact, some of the companies whose factories and products are among the biggest contributors to the problem are engaged in efforts to convince the public that global warming is not real, but merely a theory of a few crazy people when, in fact, there is nearly universal agreement in the scientific community about the existence of global warming and its seriousness."

Smith was astonished. In the pursuit of profits, the businesses of the late twentieth century had created factories and products that polluted the atmosphere to such an extent that the entire earth was threatened. Yet rather than change their behavior to reverse the threat, many businesses were doing all they could to maintain the status quo. And politicians, at least in the United States, many of whom were influenced by those very businessmen, were not addressing the problem either. He recalled what he had written in *The Wealth of Nations* about how the apparent selfish pursuit of profits by businessmen impacted society:

> . . . by directing . . . industry in such a manner as its produce may be of the greatest value, he intends only his own gain, and he is in this, as in many other cases, led by an invisible hand to promote an end which was no part of his intention. Nor is it always the worse for the society that it was no part of it. By pursuing his own interest he frequently promotes that of society more effectually than when he really intends to promote it.

Could he have been wrong? At least in this case, it seemed that the pursuit of profits, rather than promoting society, was destroying it.

–7–

Profit Maximization

Andrew parked his car in the student lot and walked over to the student center building. It was time for his second finance class, and he was eager to see where the professor would go next. He nodded hello to a woman who looked familiar—'She's in one of my classes,' he thought—and poured himself a cup of coffee at the beverage bar. After grabbing a donut and paying his tab, he headed across campus to the classroom building, munching as he walked.

The professor was already in the room when Andrew arrived, so he quickly took a seat in the front row and pulled out his notebook.

"Good afternoon," the professor began. "Our agenda today is to continue our discussion of why the goal of the for-profit firm is to maximize the wealth of its shareholders. To understand this, I have to take you back in time over 225 years."

"The modern for-profit corporation has its roots in the first Industrial Revolution that took place in Europe in the latter part of the 18th century, most notably in England. Many reasons have been advanced for why it happened then and there, but perhaps the key development was the perfection of the steam engine by James Watt in the 1760s and early 1770s. This new power source inspired people to invent steam-driven machinery that replaced manual labor in the industries of the day, at first in textiles and iron manufacturing. Entrepreneurs formed small companies to harness the new technology, and productivity and industrial output grew rapidly."

The professor turned to the white board and wrote the words: 'Adam Smith.' Turning back to the class, he asked, "Who knows who he is?" Most of the class raised their hands. The professor smiled. "Good to know some of your economics courses stuck!" He called on Andrew.

"As I recall," Andrew said, "Adam Smith was the first modern economist at the time of the Industrial Revolution."

"Correct," agreed the professor. "And what is the name of the book that established his reputation as an economist?"

When Andrew hesitated, the professor called on a man sitting at the side of the room. "Wasn't it *The Wealth of Nations?*" he offered.

"Also correct," said the professor. "Its full title was *An Inquiry Into the Nature and Causes of the Wealth of Nations,* but everyone knows it by the shorter name. And when was it published?" he asked.

Andrew had the answer this time. "1776."

"A particularly momentous year in world history, don't you think?" the professor added with a smile. He continued: "Now, *The Wealth of Nations* covered a wide range of topics that interested Adam Smith: the division of labor, the origin and use of money, commodities prices and inflation, free trade, and so on. But the topic that people most remember is Smith's analysis and conclusions on the pursuit of self interest."

"Smith observed that people tend to act in their own self-interest, and he asked if this was a bad thing in the emerging Industrial Revolution companies. His conclusion was no, that if each company tried to make the most money it could, there actually would be a good overall outcome for society."

"Now, to understand Adam Smith's world, remember that the companies he was describing were small proprietorships, not much bigger than what today we would call mom-and-pop shops. They might have as many as a few dozen workers, but they were not very complex organizations. There were no layers of management, just the owner of the business and his workers. Marketing had not yet been discovered, so companies could not distinguish their products in any meaningful way. That meant they had no pricing power and had to sell their products at the prevailing market price. The only way they could compete and make money was to keep their costs down."

"So, Smith's line of logic went like this: companies were owned by self-interested individuals who wanted to make as much money as possible. They had no ability to raise prices, so the only way they could make more money was to reduce costs. Therefore, individual self-interest would lead to goods and services being produced at the lowest cost, clearly a benefit for society."

"Smith also showed how self-interest would lead to companies bringing to market the mix of products and services demanded by consumers. If too many companies produced one item and there weren't enough buyers, the price of that item would fall. Now the least profitable companies—the ones with the highest costs—would no longer be profitable, and they would be forced to exit the market reducing the supply. On the other hand, if not enough suppliers produced an item that was in high demand, consumers would compete to buy that item and bid up its price. This would make it profitable for other companies to enter the market increasing the supply. The system was driven by people's desire to make profits. Without calling it by its modern name, Smith had described the supply-and-demand model that we still use today to characterize the behavior of free markets."

The professor paused. "One phrase from *The Wealth of Nations* has become virtually a universal shorthand for how the combined actions of all business owners lead to benefits for society, even though the business owners intend only to make money for themselves. Who knows what that phrase is?"

More than half of the students in the class raised their hands, and at least ten of them called out in unison: "the invisible hand."

–8–

Sustainability

Adam Smith looked up. He was no longer in the auditorium, but he was still not in his Kirkcaldy, Scotland home. Rather, he was in a large room with shops along all the walls. At one corner of the room was a grand stairway that led up to the next floor. In the middle of the room there were benches. People who looked like they came from every corner of the world were sitting on the benches and wandering from store to store, purchasing what was on display. Smith was in New York City. The time was the present.

Smith walked over to one of the shops and looked in the shop window. It was filled with books, mostly in English, and mostly about world problems: war, poverty, human rights, hunger, and so on. Common to all the books were the words 'United Nations' and a picture of a white map surrounded by two white olive branches on a light blue background. He turned around and saw another shop that was selling stamps. That would tell him what country he was in. When he got closer he saw that each stamp had the same words and picture as the books. 'United Nations,' Smith thought. 'What a curious name for a country!'

Back in the center of the room, a woman with a badge bearing the same picture as the books and stamps was summoning a group of people together. Smith decided to tag along. Perhaps he could learn something more about where he was. The woman raised her hand, and the group followed her to a pair of locked glass doors located to the left of the book store. She motioned to a guard on the other side of the doors, and he opened one of them allowing the group to pass through. They walked down a corridor that led to another large room, this one with a food stall in the middle. Turning right, they passed the food vendor and entered a room with two large concentric U-shaped tables facing a speaker's podium. Smith estimated there were about thirty chairs around each table, many already occupied. The woman asked the new arrivals to take any of the remaining seats. Smith chose a seat at the back of the room so he could see everything that was going on.

A man in a suit similar to the one worn by Al Gore entered the room and stepped up to the podium. "Welcome to the United Nations Symposium on Finance and Global Sustainability," he began. "We are delighted that so many of you could join us today. This is the perfect venue for our meeting as it was in this very room that much of the work of the World Commission on Environment and

Development was conducted. Of course, today we usually refer to that group as the Brundtland Commission after its chair, Dr. Gro Harlem Brundtland, the former Prime Minister of Norway and Director General of the World Health Organization."

"Perhaps a bit of history is in order," he continued. "Concern for the environment is certainly not a new issue. As early as 1832 the United States created Hot Springs Reservation in Arkansas with the intent to preserve it in its natural state, the first of what eventually would become the properties of the national park system. In 1854, Henry David Thoreau brought the appreciation of nature to the public conscience with the publication of *Walden: or, Life in the Woods*. George Perkins Marsh, considered by many the first American environmentalist, wrote about the devastating effects of deforestation in his 1864 book *Man and Nature*, even suggesting that environmental degradation was a key factor in the collapse of some ancient Mediterranean civilizations."

"The second half of the 20th century saw a growing awareness and concern about the impact of human activity on the environment. Rachael Carson's 1962 book *Silent Spring* traced the harm caused by pesticides and other chemicals. Oil spills in England and the United States in the 1960s alerted us to the damage from petroleum washing ashore. The effects of mercury on the human body became international news in 1971 as the result of a major lawsuit in Japan."

"In 1972, the United Nations held its first conference on many of these problems which we now group together under the label of sustainability. That meeting, the United Nations Conference on the Environment, was held in Stockholm and brought together for the first time delegates from around the globe, both politicians and scientists. One result of that conference was the establishment of UNEP, the United Nations Environment Programme, which is now responsible for coordinating all of the environmentally-related activities of the UN, and, in particular, encouraging sustainable development worldwide."

"Now, just what do we mean by sustainable development?" the speaker asked. "The definition that has been broadly accepted, and I am sure you all know, comes from the report of the Brundtland Commission, 'Our Common Future':

Sustainable development is development that meets the needs of the present without compromising the ability of future generations to meet their own needs."

"At the time of the Brundtland Commission, the focus of the United Nations was on environmental sustainability, making sure the earth's physical resources were not being depleted faster than they could be renewed. Today we have come to understand that we must also work to simultaneously achieve economic sustainability and social sustainability if we hope to leave a better world, or any world for that matter, to our children. Economic sustainability deals with improving standards of living, an important concern when fully half the world's population lives in poverty. Social sustainability deals with peace, crime, corruption, security, health, social unrest, and so on—the conditions that lead to conflicts, mass migration, and even terrorism. So today, sustainability is a multifaceted and complex issue. How can we reverse years of ecological damage and move toward a self-renewing environment while, at the same time, maintaining global economic growth and development, and also reducing economic, political, and social disparities? Said another way, how can we create a world in which no one is left out? And if all this cannot be done simultaneously, what is the best path for the world to take to reach these goals as we continue on what must certainly be an eternal journey?"

Adam Smith looked around at the audience, most of whom were nodding in agreement. He thought back to Al Gore's presentation. 'So, global warming is just the tip of the iceberg,' he thought. He smiled and then grimaced as he realized the irony of his little joke.

The speaker continued. "Our particular focus today is in the area of finance. For-profit businesses, operating in free markets under the rule of law, are among the greatest contributors to human well-being the world has ever known. We have done very well with the economic part of the equation, at least for roughly one third of the world's population. Unfortunately, businesses haven't done such a good job on the environmental or social issues. Their goals are financial, so it is understandable that they typically have paid little or no attention to the environment or to social justice. In fact, because sustainability does not figure into their goals, businesses have been among the greatest contributors to environmental damage, and many have set back the cause of social justice as well. The good news, however, is that businesses are potentially also the most powerful force, perhaps the only force, on the planet for reversing environmental damage and promoting social justice, for leading the way to global sustainability."

"Here at the United Nations we have begun to engage the businesses and financial institutions of the world to encourage them to integrate finance and sustainability. One mechanism is the UN Global Compact, in which over 4,000 businesses and other organizations in more than 100 countries have agreed to adopt sustainable and socially responsible policies and to report on their progress in implementing them. Another is the United Nations Environment Programme Finance Initiative, or UNEP-FI, which works with more than 160 financial institutions globally to develop and promote linkages between sustainability and financial performance."

The speaker paused and looked around the room. "We now will have presentations from representatives of the Global Compact and UNEP-FI so you can learn more of what they do, and then we will break into working groups to see how we can contribute toward their efforts."

Adam Smith reflected on what he had been hearing. Sustainability wasn't just about global warming, although that was a big concern. No, the issue was much larger and much more nuanced than he first had thought. Businesses pursuing profit maximization were indeed achieving economic success. But they were also major contributors to the world's ills. And economic success without success in preserving the environment and improving social justice was not the best result for society. At least people in the country of 'The United Nations' were taking steps to address the problem!

Smith stood up. It was time for a cup of tea. Perhaps that food stall in the next room also had some good scones. He walked to the front corner of the room and opened the door.

—9—
Shareholder Wealth ——

Andrew found the professor's description of the Industrial Revolution and Adam Smith's thinking fascinating. But several things still bothered him. He raised his hand. "I understand what you have said," he began.

"Wonderful," interjected the professor, and this elicited a laugh from the class.

Andrew blushed a bit and continued. "But here's what I don't yet understand. You said that the goal of companies is to maximize shareholder wealth, but Adam Smith was talking about profits, wasn't he? Come to think of it, that's what we learned in our economics class—that the goal of the firm is to maximize profits. Aren't we talking about two different things?"

"Excellent question," the professor replied. "In one sense we are, and in another sense we are not. This is a common point of confusion, so let's spend a few minutes clearing it up. The problem is that the meaning of the word 'profits' has changed since Adam Smith's time."

"To Adam Smith, profits were what today we would call 'economic profits.' In this definition, a firm's costs include an appropriate rate of return for the owner of the business, so if a company is profitable, it's making more than enough money to compensate its investors. Let me give you an example." He turned to the whiteboard and wrote as he spoke. "Suppose a company sells $1,000 of its products, has operating costs of $700, and the appropriate amount to return to the firm's owner is $200. Adam Smith would calculate a profit of $100." On the board he had written:

Sales revenue	$ 1,000
– operating costs	700
– return to owner	200
= Profit	100

"However, modern accounting systems define profits to exclude anything that goes to the firm's owners. Today that same company's profits would be reported as:"

Sales revenue	$ 1,000
– operating costs	700
= Profit	300

"Now consider another company that sells $1,000 of its products, but has operating costs of $900. The appropriate amount to return to the firm's owner is still $200. By modern accounting standards, this is a profitable firm." He wrote:

Sales revenue	$ 1,000
– operating costs	900
= Profit	100

"But not by Adam Smith's definition:"

Sales revenue	$ 1,000
– operating costs	900
– return to owner	200
= Loss	–100

"Adam Smith's calculation shows that this company fell $100 short in bringing in enough money both to pay its operating costs and to return the appropriate amount to its owner. Note, on the other hand, that the modern accounting calculation completely ignores whether the owner was properly compensated for his investment. So, as you can see, today the term 'profits' can mean two entirely different things."

"No wonder I had such a hard time in accounting!" said a student in the back row, and the class broke out in laughter.

The professor smiled. "Now, economists like to use the old definition of profits—economic profits—just as Adam Smith did. So, for them, the concept of 'maximizing profits' still translates to maximizing the returns to the firm's owners. That's why your economics professor taught you it was the goal of the firm. However, because today's for-profit corporations are required to prepare their financial reports according to modern accounting rules, the profit numbers that investors see tell them nothing about whether the company is providing an appropriate return to its shareholders. We need another way to measure what a company is giving to its owners."

"Makes sense," said Andrew, and the class murmured in agreement.

The professor resumed his train of thought. "There are other reasons why the term 'profits' fell out of favor in finance when talking about the goal of the firm. For one thing, accounting profits are calculated by applying a series of rules that are legislated by the accounting profession. Just like in the Congress, these 'laws' are the result of lots of negotiation and compromise. The rules change from time to time as old rules are modified or scrapped and as new rules are created. In some cases, there are choices in how the rules may be applied—you may recall the choice between the LIFO and FIFO inventory methods or between straight-line and accelerated deprecation. So, there is no reason to believe that accounting rules are 'correct' in any absolute sense."

"For another thing, profits refer to a period of time: this year's profits, next year's profits, and so on. Which one are we talking about? Which one should we maximize? What if increasing this year's profits meant that next year's profits would be reduced? Would this be a benefit for the firm's owners? It turns out there is no way to determine this within the accounting system."

"There are two more problems with accounting profits that make them the wrong thing to maximize. First, in finance we've learned that a company's value comes from its cash flows, that is, its ability to bring in more cash than it spends. But cash flows don't always equal the accounting measures of profit. By the way, understanding cash flows is so important that we'll spend a lot of time looking at them throughout this course. Second, profits tell us nothing about risk. There are low-risk investments such as insured savings accounts, and there are investments that have lots of risk—investing in a new startup company for example. The evidence is that risk is important to investors when they evaluate a company, yet the profit numbers essentially ignore it."

"So, finance people searched for a new measure of what a company was returning to its owners. The new measure had to be unaffected by accounting rules, not limited to only one year, based on cash flows, and include information about risk. The best measure—in fact the *only* measure we know of—is the growth of the value of the company. For publicly-owned and traded corporations, this is the firm's stock price. A corporation's stock price is set by investors in the financial markets as a result of their analyses of the company's prospects. Investors should look past the amount and timing of accounting profits to cash flows and should take risk into account in their evaluation. In fact, anything important to investors should be part of their analyses, so it turns out that stock price is quite an inclusive number."

"Another way to say this is that the value of the company to its shareholders is the one portion of the shareholders' wealth the company's managers can influence. The company does the best it can for its owners when it acts to maximize the company's share price. And this is why in finance we say that the goal of the firm is to maximize shareholders' wealth."

10

Suboptimization

Stepping through the door, Adam Smith found himself back in the parlour of his Kirkcaldy, Scotland home. He looked around. Everything seemed to be just as he had left it. Spotting a decorative plate on the mantelpiece of the great fireplace, he remembered that he was looking for tea and scones. Gingerly, he opened the door to the kitchen, fully expecting some strange time and place to lie beyond. But he found that the door did indeed lead to his kitchen, and he let out a sigh of relief. It was good to be home.

Smith lit a fire, put up a kettle of water, and sat down at the table in the kitchen waiting for the water to boil. He tried to wrap his mind around the events of the last few hours. Or, was it the last few days? Or, weeks? He wasn't sure. There was no one in the house with him that he could ask. Then he had an idea. Getting up, he went back into the parlour, and then on through the far door to his study. He walked over to the west-facing windows. It was late afternoon—where was the sun in the sky? Further to the north? Further to the south? It didn't seem like the sun was in a much different position than the last time he had looked out that window, just before his adventures had begun. Perhaps not much time had passed after all.

Smith sat down at his desk and took out a piece of paper. He uncovered the inkwell, and dipped the tip of a pen into the dark liquid. Then he began to write down some of what he had seen and heard. He wrote about the auditorium in which Al Gore had been lecturing, including the technology that he didn't understand. He described the meeting room in the United Nations building and the people who were attending the conference.

A twinge in his stomach reminded Smith that he had not yet had his tea. He put down his pen and went back to the kitchen where he poured the now boiling water into a tea pot. After swirling the hot water around several times to warm the pot, he poured the water out. Then he added loose tea leaves and filled the pot with hot water. Placing a tea cosy over the pot to keep it warm while the tea brewed, he went to the cupboard and took out three scones, eating the first one on the way back to the tea pot. He placed a cloth over a tea cup to act as a strainer and poured the brew through the cloth into the cup. Satisfied that no tea leaves had penetrated the cloth, he carried his cup of tea and the remaining two scones back to the study.

Taking a sip of tea, Smith reread what he had written so far. He had described the people and places he had seen, but he had not written anything about what they were talking about. He took out another piece of paper, dipped his pen into the inkwell, and began writing again, this time attempting to capture the content and logic of what he had heard. One hour passed. Then another. He had become so engrossed in his writing that he had completely ignored the two scones sitting on the corner of the desk. Hungrily, he took a big bite of the one nearest to him.

Smith finished the scone and thought about what he had written. The common thread was something called 'sustainability.' At the minimum, that meant ensuring that the earth and its inhabitants continued to survive. At a deeper level, it meant improving the lives of all people. A light bulb turned on in Smith head. Sustainability was the way the people of the early 21st century were stating the ultimate goals of society.

Smith recalled the words he had written about businessmen in *The Theory of Moral Sentiments*:

> ... in spite of their natural selfishness and rapacity, though they mean only their own conveniency, though the sole end which they propose from the labours of all the thousands whom they employ, be the gratification of their own vain

and insatiable desires, they divide with the poor the produce of all their improvements. They are led by an invisible hand to make nearly the same distribution of the necessaries of life, which would have been made, had the earth been divided into equal portions among all its inhabitants, and thus without intending it, without knowing it, advance the interest of the society.

At the beginning of the third millennium, that didn't seem to be happening. Businessmen were not dividing with the poor the produce of all their improvements. The necessaries of life were not being distributed to all the earth's inhabitants, certainly not equally. And beyond that, businesses were continuing to damage an environment that had already become quite fragile. What had gone wrong? Was his conclusion that an invisible hand would guide profit maximizing businesses to act for the benefit of society incorrect?

Sustainability had at least three aspects: economic, environmental, and social. Perhaps the problem was that he had addressed only the economics and ignored the other two. That would imply that maximizing profits did not always produce the best for society, that it was an incomplete goal for firms to pursue.

Smith knew he had much more to learn before he could answer his fundamental question: was profit maximization wrong? He had many other unanswered questions as well. From his short glimpse into the world of the future, he could see that it was a much more complex place than the world he knew. Exactly what had changed? How did it get that way? How did thinking about the role and goal of the business firm evolve between now and then? He wondered if he would ever find out. Hopefully the muses that had transported him to the future would return so he could learn the answers to his questions!

Smith decided to take a walk in the garden. Perhaps the fresh air would help his thinking. Picking up the last scone, he walked across his study and opened the door to the parlour.

11

Agency

The weekend flew by for Andrew. He spent most of the day Saturday turning the second bedroom of the apartment he shared with Jennifer into a den and office where he could study. Then on Sunday, he read and took notes on the assigned chapters in his finance textbook before taking a break and catching the second half of the ball game on TV. Now it was Monday and time for his next finance class. Excited, Andrew arrived fifteen minutes early.

The professor began the class with some administrative comments about the course syllabus. Then he returned to the subject of the goal of the firm. "In our last class we talked about how shareholder wealth supplanted profits as the goal of the for-profit company," he began. "Now when I talked about maximizing shareholder wealth, I thought I saw a few frowns on some of your faces. Would anyone who reacted that way be willing to share why you did so?"

"I was probably one of those who made a face," said a man in the center of the room. "Here's what bothers me: I don't see why the shareholders should get everything. Doesn't a firm have to do the best it can for its customers and employees as well as its shareholders if it is going to succeed?"

The woman sitting to Andrew's left agreed. "I was thinking the same thing. If a company maximizes what it gives to its shareholders, doesn't it necessarily reduce what it can give to its customers and employees? And wouldn't the quality of its products suffer as well. I mean, there's only so much to go around. The company's resources aren't infinite."

"I was concerned about a different implication," volunteered another woman. "People who can afford to own stock are often the richest people in society. I guess I am uncomfortable with a business goal that favors those people who are already well off at the expense of those who are not."

"My concern goes beyond that," said another student. "Managers have lots of power compared to shareholders. What worries me is that they seem to take too much of the firm's profits and don't leave as much as they should for the shareholders."

"Excellent observations," said the professor. "These are indeed concerns that have been raised about shareholder wealth maximization. However, it turns out that none of these concerns make maximizing shareholder wealth wrong as the goal of the firm. Let me take them one at a time."

"The first concern was that maximizing shareholder wealth could result in other stakeholders being short-changed." He nodded in acknowledgment to the man in the center of the room who had raised the topic. Then he surveyed the faces of the entire class. "Who knows what a 'stakeholder' is?" he asked. Several hands shot up, and the professor called on a woman in the third row.

"Isn't a stakeholder anyone who is affected by the actions of a company?" she offered.

"Exactly," the professor confirmed. "And that definition isn't limited to businesses. The same definition holds for any organization, regardless of how it is organized. Think about this university, for example. You are all stakeholders of this school, as am I, as are all the university's other employees, alumni, donors, neighbors, and so on. For a business, the typical stakeholders are the company's employees, suppliers, customers, lenders, investors, neighbors, and even the government."

"Now, management faces a constant series of decisions about how to divide up the revenues from selling the company's products. Finance theory says that the goal is to give as much as possible to the shareholders, but there are realistic limits to how far a company can go in that direction. For example, if a company didn't pay a fair price for raw materials, some of its suppliers would deliver shoddy inventory—if they were willing to do business with the company at all. If it didn't pay reasonable wages, employees wouldn't care very much about the company and wouldn't do good work or would leave. Pretty quickly the word would get out that this is a company that makes poor-quality products and doesn't treat its suppliers and employees well, and it would lose customers to its competitors. The way to give the most to shareholders is to find a balance in which all stakeholders feel they are fairly compensated—not overpaid, but not underpaid either. It is not easy, but it's one of the key jobs of management. So, shareholder wealth maximization is quite consistent with fairness to stakeholders."

The professor continued. "Now your second concern was that maximizing shareholder wealth could result in poor quality products. In fact it's just the opposite. The globalization of business over the past several decades has intensified the competitive picture for all companies. Today, a business that doesn't produce high-quality products doesn't survive for very long." He paused for a minute, then asked, "How many of you own a television set or audio system produced by an American company?" No one raised a hand.

"Your third concern was that stock is owned primarily by the wealthy, therefore the goal of the firm rewards the rich. That may have been true fifty years ago, but it isn't quite as true today. Today, most stock is actually owned by people like you and me, as part of our retirement plans." He opened a folder he had brought to class and searched for a newspaper article. Finding it, he pulled it out and looked up at the class. "By the end of 2005, fully half of all households in the United States owned stock in corporations. I don't have the latest figures, but I believe the number has grown somewhat since then. Now, I'd be the first to admit that there are rich people who own lots of stock, while the average stockholder owns far fewer shares. But the reality is that when we talk of maximizing shareholder wealth, we are talking about benefitting more than half of the population, not just a few rich people."

"Finally, you were concerned about the ability of managers to reward themselves at the expense of shareholders. This is indeed a real concern. Back in the day of Adam Smith, at the time of the Industrial Revolution, a company's owner was its manager, so the problem didn't exist. Today, of course, most large companies are not run by their shareholder-owners, but by professional managers, effectively hired by the shareholders to maximize the value of their investment. The problem you speak of is the result of the modern separation of ownership and control."

"In finance we call this concern the 'agency problem,' and there is an entire branch of finance theory and practice devoted to it. You may have come across the term 'agent' in your business law course. In legal terminology an agent is someone who works professionally for another, for example a doctor, or a lawyer, or an accountant. The agent is responsible for giving the person he or she works for—the agent's 'principal'—his or her best effort with no conflict of interest."

"As we use the terms in finance, a company's managers are agents of the shareholders who are the principals. The shareholder-principals hire the manager-agents to maximize the value of their investment in the firm, and they want the managers to work in their best interests. But of course, the personal goals of the managers often differ from those of the shareholders. So the managers often do what is best for themselves, regardless of whether it maximizes shareholder wealth."

A student raised her hand. "Isn't that what happened at Enron?" she asked.

"Yes," agreed the professor. "For starters, the managers of Enron arranged deals that paid millions of dollars to themselves, their families, and their friends, all at a time when the company was losing money. To cover up the company's losses, they reported assets on their books at inflated values, including some that didn't even exist, and hid hundreds of millions of dollars of debt and losses in 'offshore' subsidiaries. The fraudulent accounting fooled the markets, and the value of Enron stock rose. Then, at the peak of the market, Enron's managers sold millions of dollars of their personal stock making even more huge profits for themselves."

"Now, Enron is an extreme example. It's true that every once in a while something egregious like Enron happens. But the agency problem exists even in companies with none of the fraud and excesses of Enron. Managers simply have different motivations than shareholders. For example, they spend a relatively short time in each job and hence tend to favor decisions that pay off before they move on to their next position over decisions with a longer-term payoff. They often have significant control over their pay and perquisites independent of what shareholders might consider the fair value of their compensation. They typically can limit the information that shareholders receive about the company which permits them to make decisions that favor themselves without having to be held accountable. Their attitudes toward risk often differ from those of the shareholders. So, the issue is not to prevent managers from thinking about themselves—this is normal human behavior. The real issue is how to align managers' motivations with those of the shareholders, so when they do act for themselves they are also acting in the best interests of the shareholders."

"So, you see, shareholder wealth maximization really is the correct goal for the firm. The real problem in today's world is ensuring that managers actually do it!"

12

Frankenstein

On the other side of the door was a parlour, but it was not Adam Smith's. Rather, it was significantly larger and quite a bit more opulent than the parlour of Smith's home. The wall covering was of a fleur-de-lis design, and the large paintings were mostly of landscapes, not ancestors such as those that lined the walls of Smith's parlour. Outside the window was a great lawn that sloped down to a large lake. Smith was in Cologny, Switzerland. The year was 1816.

There were five people in the room. A young couple was sitting on the sofa opposite the door where Smith had entered. Another young man was sitting on a chair facing the couple while a second woman, even younger looking than the first, sat on a love seat next to the sofa. A third man, slightly older, was pacing back and forth in front of the large, ornate fireplace. Smith guessed the men were in their mid-to-late twenties. The women looked barely twenty years old.

The man sitting on the sofa looked up and spoke with obvious annoyance. "Is there no relief from this horrid weather?" he asked. "We came here to spend the summer! The summer, not the winter! Why will not the weather cooperate? It rains each morning and each afternoon, not the rain of summer that caresses the flowers and imbues a leisurely stroll by the lake with laughter and romance, but a cold rain that chills to the bone. We have been here a fortnight already, but we have hardly left the villa."

The man who was pacing back and forth responded. "Then dear Percy, the time is nigh for us to engage in an activity more appropriate for the parlour than the lakeside path." He reached into a sac he had brought with him into the room and withdrew a book.

"Come now George," Percy Bysshe Shelly retorted. "Your idea of something new is to read a book? We have been doing little else since we arrived at this god-awful place."

"Ah," George Byron replied. "But this is not just any book. It is the perfect book for this 'god-awful place'." He mimicked the tone of Shelly's complaint as he said the last three words.

"And what book might that be?" asked the younger woman, with clear interest.

"My ever curious Claire," acknowledged Byron. He adopted a conspiratorial tone of voice. "It is known as: *Fantasmagoriana, or a Collection of Stories of Apparitions, Specters, Spirits, Phantoms, etc.* It is a book of ghost stories. This copy is translated from the original German. We shall read it in French."

"How perfect!" Claire Clairmont enthused.

"Yes, perfect," added Mary Shelly. "Thank god we will have something different to do tonight." Turning to George, she added with a wink, "Will the good Lord Byron be transformed into the evil Lord Byron when the light of dawn peeks through yon window?"

Byron grinned broadly. "Only the chimes of the clock will tell us whether we remain unchanged in the darkness of this night. Only tomorrow will we know whether this night was merely another night of utter boredom or whether we will have discovered something new deep within each of us."

They took turns reading pages from the book with great enthusiasm. They voiced the words of the various characters and acted out parts of each story with obvious joy. They laughed and joked and continued through the night with hardly a break. It was quite a welcome change from the depression of the previous two weeks.

As he listened, Adam Smith thought how fortunate he was to be able to understand the French they were speaking. From 1763 to 1766, prior to beginning work on *The Wealth of Nations*, Smith had been employed to tutor Henry Scott, the wealthy young Duke of Buccleuch and Queensberry, and to take him on the grand tour of Europe. By the time they had returned to Scotland, Smith was quite competent in French and in German as well.

As dawn broke, Byron issued a challenge to the other four. "These stories are good, but we can do better. We can do much better. We are smart. We are educated. We are well read. We have imaginations that compare most favourably to the authors of these tales. I hereby challenge us all to a duel—a duel of words. We shall each write our own ghost story. Whose story will be the best? Whose story will send chills up our spines? Whose story will make us afraid to close our eyes when sleep finally overcomes our literary exertions?"

Three days and three sleepless nights flew by, although for Adam Smith it seemed like a mere blink of an eye. John Polidori, the third man present—who, in addition to being Byron's friend was his personal physician—warned more than once of the consequences of a lack of sleep, however he was gleefully ignored, and even he joined in. The five had taken up Lord Byron's challenge with gusto, and the results were astonishing. Each had produced one or more excellent story ideas, and a few were well along in their development. However, two efforts clearly stood out from the rest.

Mary Shelly had written the outline of a story that would become the basis for her novel *Frankenstein, The Modern Prometheus*. Lord Byron had written the beginnings of a story based on the vampire legends of Eastern Europe, a story John Polidori would later expand into *The Vampyre*.

The one person who was tired was Adam Smith. He had been fascinated by what he had just witnessed, although he couldn't quite see its relevance to his quest. Why had he been there? He turned and walked out of the room. However, instead of returning to his Scottish home, he found himself standing outside a theater on a city street. In the display window next to the theater door was a poster identifying the title of the play as 'Frankenstein' and containing an illustration of a deformed giant threatening a middle-aged man who was running away from the creature with a fearful expression on his face. Smith was in London, England. It was four years later, 1820.

A young couple was standing in front of the theater in conversation with an older man. Smith recognized them as Mary and Percy Bysshe Shelly, the young couple he had observed in Switzerland. Mary Shelly was speaking to the older man. "I must thank you deeply, Sir Walter, for your kind public words about my story. I am certain they have contributed to the desire of people to learn about it."

Sir Walter Scott smiled at Mary. "I do you no favours my dear. My words reflect what I see and feel just as, I am sure, do yours. Your story is remarkably well written and demonstrates a level of originality not often seen these days in the West End. It has depth, and may be interpreted on many levels. I, for one, can see more than one message in it. Pray, tell me which is the message you most wished to convey?"

"We are in the midst of a great scientific revolution," Mary replied. "Will the creations of the most brilliant scientists of our age be used wisely, or will we become victims of our own progress? Will the modern life we create improve the conditions under which men live, or might it ultimately destroy them?"

Sir Walter Scott nodded with interest. "Do tell me more," he asked Mary.

When she did not immediately reply, Percy became impatient. "Mary is far too modest," he said. "There is so much more to the story. The central message is, indeed, that no matter how good their intentions, people cannot predict how their grand designs will be corrupted. But this applies to every realm of life, not just science. Consider the French Revolution. The revolutionaries gave their lives for freedom from the oppressive rule of Louis XVI and Marie Antoinette. They thought they had given birth to a new era in the history of France, yet look how quickly the Revolution descended into the Terror of Robespierre, then Napoleon, and now there is a monarchy again."

"Or, consider the rapidly accelerating industrialization of England," Percy continued. "Adam Smith and David Ricardo tell us why this is good for mankind and good for society. We all will have a greater level of material goods, they say, hence we all will live better lives. But Mary is warning us that inside every businessman resides the heart of Victor Frankenstein, that every business carries the seeds of a dangerous experiment. Who knows what horror might emerge. And once the horror is unleashed, can the damage ever fully be reversed? Is it possible to create a new industrial order without causing hardship for some, perhaps for many? When man devotes his labor to a company owned and run by others, does he not lose a portion of his soul? Mary's voice rings out loud and clear to warn us all."

Mary looked at her husband and smiled appreciatively. "Percy is always so brilliant at seeing meaning where others cannot, so certainly I will not deny his interpretations."

Adam Smith now understood why he had visited Switzerland those four years ago. His head was reeling, and he needed a drink. He walked over to a pub next to the theater and opened the door.

13

Externalities

Andrew parked his car and walked quickly around the corner towards the café. He was meeting Jennifer for lunch before going to his afternoon finance class, and he didn't want to keep her waiting. It was a beautiful, warm fall day, and the colors of the trees and sky seemed especially vibrant.

Jennifer waived her arm to catch his attention as Andrew came into view, and he made his way over to her table, leaned down, and gave her a kiss. She returned the kiss and smiled broadly. "It's such a wonderful day that I thought we should eat outside and enjoy the weather. Besides," she added, "the people watching is so much better out here than inside."

"Sold!" responded Andrew with a grin. He sat down and began studying the menu. "Sometimes, I wonder why I even look at this menu. We've eaten here so many times now that I feel I know it by heart."

"The day you don't read the menu is the day they'll change it." She laughed. "You know what I think? I think that your reading the menu every time we're here is the reason is has stayed the same for so long!"

Andrew laughed at the implication and put the menu down. Seeing that neither Jennifer nor Andrew were reading their menus, a waitress came over and took their orders. Then they began to chat about what their mornings had been like.

"I had a really unpleasant experience on my way to work today," Jennifer said.

Andrew frowned with concern. "Like what?"

"Well, you know that on my way in I usually stop at that coffee shop near my office—their coffee is so much better than the sludge that comes out of the machines inside our building."

"Right," nodded Andrew.

"Well, there's supposed to be no smoking inside the shop. There's even a sign on one of the walls, right by the door to the restrooms. But today the man in front of me on line was smoking, and no one from the shop was telling him to stop. So, I asked him if he would put his cigarette out."

"And . . .?"

"And he got really nasty and told me that it was none of my business and that if it bothered me I could just leave and go to some other coffee shop. So, I told him he was a really inconsiderate person—I think I used a slightly stronger word—and we got into a bit of a shouting match. We must have been so loud that the people who worked there heard us because a couple of them quickly intervened and stopped the argument."

"And then . . .?"

"And then they told him to leave. But as they ushered him out he kept pointing at me and telling me that I should have kept my mouth shut and it was none of my business. At least the fellow behind the counter apologized to me."

"I'm really sorry," said Andrew sincerely. "You must have been a little scared."

"More than a little. I mean, he was much bigger than I am, and boy did he have a temper. I stayed in the shop for another fifteen minutes just to be sure he wasn't waiting outside to accost me again."

"You should have called me. I would have come right over."

Jennifer smiled for the first time since she began her story. "Thanks. I know you would have." The look of concern returned to her face. "But it *was* my business, wasn't it?" She looked at Andrew for support. "I mean, it *was* my business that he was smoking in a no smoking area, right?"

"Of course it was your business. For two reasons. First, you had the right to expect the smoke-free environment you were promised by the shop's policies. You were simply being a responsible customer when you pointed out the man was smoking, although . . ." He paused for a moment. ". . . although, it might have been a better strategy to have directed your complaint to the employees and let them handle it from the start."

"I suppose," she agreed, "although he probably would have yelled at me anyway for turning him in." She paused for a moment and looked down at the table, reflecting back on the incident. Then she looked back up at Andrew. "You said there were two reasons."

"The other reason is the problem of second-hand smoke. That man was harming the health of everyone around him. So of course it was your business. In fact, it was the business of everyone inside the shop. You were the brave one who confronted the issue, but everyone else in the room should have complained as well."

"Thanks. Fortunately no one here is smoking," Jennifer observed, "so we can enjoy the wonderful fresh air." She smiled lovingly at Andrew. ". . . and the wonderful company," she added.

"And the good food!" said Andrew as the waitress delivered their sandwiches.

For the next thirty minutes they ate, talked, and commented on the people passing by. Then Andrew paid the check, gave Jennifer a kiss, and drove to the university for his class.

As he drove, Andrew kept thinking about Jennifer's experience that morning. Why would that man smoke where it wasn't permitted? If he knew about the effects of second-hand smoke—and who didn't these days—why would he smoke around other people regardless of where he was? Because he could? Because it was macho? Because he just didn't care about anyone else? Because there was no penalty for doing so? Before he knew it, Andrew was entering the university parking lot. Five minutes later he was in the classroom.

When his finance professor began the class by asking if anyone had questions about the material they had covered so far, Andrew raised his hand.

"My fiancée had an incident this morning involving second-hand smoke, and it got me thinking about what we have said about the goal of the firm being to maximize shareholder wealth. I guess the equivalent of second-hand smoke for a company is the smoke from its factories. What's to prevent a company from polluting the air, or the water, or the land for that matter? I mean, it may be more profitable for a company just to dump its waste than to pay to clean it up or dispose of it in a responsible way. If that's the case, maybe shareholder wealth maximization isn't such a good thing."

"You are talking about what we call 'externalities'," the professor replied. "An externality is anything that affects us that is caused by the actions of others and has no price or cost attached to it. They can be both good or bad, that is, positive or negative. A positive externality is a benefit we don't pay for. For example, as more and more people are vaccinated against a disease, the probability of you or me catching it decreases. We are healthier, but we don't pay for it directly. What your fiancée experienced was a negative externality, damage that we bear that we don't get paid for. When we're around second-hand smoke, we become less healthy, but no one compensates us for our loss."

"The finance question becomes how much should a company pay to prevent creating a negative externality like pollution. Unfortunately, in most cases the answer isn't that obvious. For starters, there is often no way to determine how much spending is the correct amount. As you pointed out, it is costly not to pollute. Therefore, companies face a tradeoff between reducing pollution and producing their products at the lowest cost. So what is the correct balance between pollution and meeting economic needs? I'm sure there is one, but there is no formula that points to the answer."

"There's another problem. Suppose a company in a highly competitive market decided to spend money to reduce pollution while their competitors chose not to. The company's competitors would be able consistently to undercut its prices and would eventually put it out of business. Competitive pressures force every company to be very careful in spending money that doesn't directly improve their products or customer service."

"As a result, the conclusion of the finance community is that these questions must be resolved by society, not any one company, and the vehicle for society to do this is government. For example, if the government passed a law mandating maximum permissible pollution levels and specifying hefty fines for violations, these concerns would be addressed. There would be a clear and defined cost to polluting. Companies would know how much reduction in pollution is the accepted amount. And the requirement to reach those levels would fall equally on all companies."

"So you see, the goal of shareholder wealth maximization remains valid. It's government's job to ensure a level playing field and to require companies to do what society has decided it wants."

–14–

Communism

There really was a pub on the other side of the door. Smith looked around and found an unoccupied table near a window. He sat down with a sigh and surveyed the room. The pub looked like every other pub he recalled: small, paneled with dark wood, and not particularly well lit. Smith was in London, England. The year was 1871.

He motioned for the bar maid but she ignored him. He waived at her again—no response. Then he recalled that others seemed unable to see or hear him, so he walked over to the bar and poured himself a pint of his favorite bitter. Smith returned to his table and took a hearty swallow. It felt good to sit down for a change. He stared absent-mindedly at two men who were throwing darts at a target on the far wall. However, his trance soon was broken by the noise coming from the next table.

A group of men was in the midst of a loud discussion. At first Smith thought that they were having an argument, but he soon realized that it was more of an intellectual give-and-take. The scene was familiar and reminded him of the many late-night, philosophical discussions he had participated in while a student at Glasgow and Oxford. He took another sip of his beer and tried to ignore the conversation, which, after all, he was not a party to, but it was too loud and he found that he heard every word.

"My point," a man with long grey hair and bushy beard was saying, "is that we must distinguish between the means of production and the relations of production. If we do not make this distinction, we cannot see the truth of what is happening."

"And just what is the distinction you are making, Karl?" asked the man sitting to his right.

Karl Marx glanced at his questioner. His voice became firmer. "The means of production are the inputs that have been recognized and described for many years now by those who call themselves economists, beginning with Adam Smith and David Ricardo: land, labor, machinery, and so on." Smith turned his head slightly when he heard his name mentioned and began to listen more intently. "The problem is that they go no further in their descriptions of economic activity."

"And 'the relations of production'?" asked the same man.

Marx continued, "By this I mean the social relationships of the workers: which groups they belong to and how they interact in and with these groups at work and elsewhere."

"But there is more to it than that," interrupted the dark-haired man with an equally long but pointed beard sitting across from Karl Marx.

"Yes, yes, Friedrich," Marx replied. "The relations of production must also include the relationship between the worker and his work. This is the crux of the matter. Consider the craftsman who lovingly turns a piece of wood into his product. He puts his heart and soul into his work. The product reflects the skill, indeed the emotions of the worker. It is his, and he cares for it as if it were his child. It is very different for a factory worker who operates a machine that makes many copies each week of only one small part of a product. He plays only a small role in the completed product. Whatever skill he has is directed to the machine, not to the product. He has given up the ability to make the product his own. Indeed, compared to the craftsman, he has given up much of his ability to transform his world. He has lost a portion of his soul! And it must follow that he has become alienated from his work and lost all feeling for the company that employs him."

The concept of alienation hadn't occurred to Adam Smith previously although he had worried about one effect of repetitive work in *The Wealth of Nations*:

The man whose whole life is spent in performing a few simple operations ... generally becomes as stupid and ignorant as it is possible for a human creature to become.

The third man at the table spoke up. "But if workers are so alienated from their employers, why do they stay? Do they have no choice? Even more perplexing, why do others leave the crafts where they toil with their hands to enter this soul-less world?"

This time is was Friedrich Engels whose voice rose in intensity. "At every point in history, the ruling classes have determined and controlled the beliefs that have been accepted by all of society. Since the ideology of any society is designed by its rulers, it is no surprise that it reflects the interests of those in power. Why do peasants everywhere not revolt against their oppressors? It is because they have been taught from the time they were born that society's roles must be what they are. Their role is to be subservient to others. And they believe it, at serious cost to themselves. Workers do not leave the factories because they have been told it is where they belong."

"And the consequence of this is that the workers are exploited by their capitalist masters," Karl Marx added. "The workers lose their ability to make a living outside of industry. They have no choice left but to work for whatever wages the factory owners will pay. Of course, the capitalist will never pay his workers the full value of their labor, for if he did, he could not make a profit. He must be able to sell his products for more than what he pays to produce them. The very basis of capitalism therefore, comes from paying workers less than the value they add to the company's products. It is the capitalists who keep the surplus value. We end up with two classes of people in society: a small, wealthy capitalist class and a large, barely surviving working class. We end up with a very unequal distribution of resources and wealth."

Friedrich Engels added, "And of course, this explains perfectly the horrible working conditions we find in the factories of England. The capitalists have no motivation at all to make any change and every motivation to keep things as they currently are."

"A truth that you shared with the world so eloquently in your superb book," complimented Marx.

The discussion reminded Adam Smith of a sentence from *The Wealth of Nations*:

> Masters are always and every where in a sort of tacit, but constant and uniform combination, not to raise the wages of labour.

The third man had a very resigned look on his face. "Is there no hope then for society?" he asked.

"Oh, there is hope," replied Marx. "This will not last. I am certain of it."

"How so?"

"Society originated as small tribes in which there were no class distinctions, and there were so few resources they were shared by all. However, as tribes clustered together and populations grew, social classes developed. At the extreme there were masters and servants, monarchs and slaves. Where there had once been absolute equality, there was now extreme inequality. Here in England, society has been moving back toward greater equality since the Magna Carta in 1215. Power devolved from the sole monarch to feudal lords. Now much of that power has shifted once again, from a landed nobility to the new capitalist class. But history is not yet over. The internal contradictions of capitalism will destroy it as workers eventually understand their plight and rise up in revolution against their capitalist masters. The working class will become the grave diggers of capitalism."

"And then? What comes next?"

"The workers will themselves own the means of production and will work for themselves. With no more capitalists there will be no more social classes. A classless society will emerge, governed by the people themselves. True equality will have arrived once again, just as in the earliest tribal days."

"But what will change the subservient behavior of the working class? How will they learn of this opportunity you describe?"

Marx took a deep breath. "It is people like ourselves who understand the course of history who must tell the truth to them and show them there is a better way."

Adam Smith turned back to his beer and took a deep draught. His head was spinning, and not just from the dense cigarette smoke in the pub. Had the pursuit of profits led to a dramatically unequal society, one ready for revolution? Was this the effect of business on society? He quickly finished his drink and headed for the door to get some fresh air.

15

—— *Dinner* ——

The sun was setting as Andrew pulled his car into the assigned parking space in front of the apartment. After his finance class, he and several of his classmates had gotten together in the student lounge to work on homework problems and to prepare a case that was to be discussed at the next class. The work was fun, and the afternoon flew by. Before Andrew knew it, it was time to call it a day.

Jennifer met him at the door. She was wearing a dress and heels, not the jeans and t-shirt he expected. Had he forgotten about some event they had to go to that night? Before he could ask her what was up, he saw that the living room lights were dimmed and there were candles on the dining table which was set for two people. They weren't going out!

Andrew kissed his fiancée. Then, saying he would only be a minute, he went into the bedroom where he cleaned himself up and put on good clothes. He splashed on some of the cologne that Jennifer had bought for his last birthday and rejoined her in the living room. She handed him a glass of wine and picked up a second glass for herself.

"What's the occasion?" asked Andrew with a bemused smile on his face. "Not that we need an occasion, of course!" he quickly added. His look turned to one of curiosity. "Is there an occasion?"

"Not so much an occasion as a transition," answered Jennifer. "You made a big decision to leave your job and go back to school for your MBA degree. I think it's time to celebrate this new chapter in our lives. Actually, I was thinking of celebrating on the evening of your first day of school, but, as I recall, you had some doubts. So, I decided to wait until I knew that you were sure it was the right decision. Now I know. Your enthusiasm every time you come home tells me so. I'm very happy for you and very proud of you."

"You are amazing!" said Andrew, and he gave her a big hug, almost spilling her wine.

Jennifer led him to the table and motioned for him to sit. She put her glass down and turned on some romantic music. Then she disappeared into the kitchen and returned with Andrew's favorite dish. She sat down and raised her glass. "To the future!"

"To the future!" Andrew repeated as he lifted his glass and tapped it gently against hers. The wine glasses made a particularly dull sound as they touched. "Some day we will be able to afford good wine glasses," he promised.

"You know I don't care about that," Jennifer responded. "I just hope we are always as happy as we are tonight."

The conversation over dinner was warm and intimate. They talked about their hopes and dreams. They spoke of their parents and siblings. They joked about how many children they would have and what to name them.

When they had finished eating, they cleared the table together. Then Jennifer brought out a cake inscribed with the same message as her toast, 'To the future!' She went over to the coffee table, brought back a present, and placed it in front of Andrew. "To the future, our future," she said, "and to success in your MBA program and your professional life."

"You shouldn't have," said Andrew with a grateful look on his face.

"Go ahead, open it," urged Jennifer.

Andrew removed the ribbon and wrapping paper and opened the box. He looked up at Jennifer with amazement when he saw the old book. Gently taking it out of the box, he read the title out loud, *"An Inquiry Into the Nature and Causes of the Wealth of Nations."* Adam Smith's book. "This is amazing!" He jumped up and gave Jennifer a big hug. "Where in the world did you find this?" he asked.

"At that monthly flea market I like to go to. I got it from a book vendor I hadn't seen before. Actually, I was lucky to find it. I missed seeing it the first time I looked at the books on the table. Do you like it?"

"Like it? I love it! Thank you *so* much," exclaimed Andrew, repeating, "This is amazing!" He turned the book over several times studying its leather binding. "This must be a really old edition."

"I couldn't find any date in it other than 1776. Wasn't that the year Smith wrote it? I can't believe it could be true, but maybe we got lucky and this is a first edition."

Andrew looked through the first few pages for another date but he too could not find one. "That would be incredible. Some day we'll have to take it to an expert and find out. But regardless, thank you *so* much. This means so much to me. *You* mean so much to me." He gave her another hug and a kiss.

For the next fifteen minutes Andrew talked excitedly about what he was learning in his finance class, particularly how the goal and decision-making process of the modern company could be traced directly back to Adam Smith and *The Wealth of Nations*. "That makes your gift so extra special." But as he went on, Jennifer began to frown. "What's wrong?" he asked.

"I'm having trouble reconciling something," answered Jennifer. "I hear what you are saying about the goal of companies being a financial one, and how the 'invisible hand' of the marketplace harnesses the self interest of business owners to produce a good result for society. But that result is only financial. Of course I agree that providing products and services and jobs and incomes to people is very important, but there are other things that are important as well. Just this morning, there was an article in the paper about how increased greenhouse gas emissions from businesses are melting the polar icecaps and how many millions of people could lose their homes if sea levels rose. And there was that program on TV the other night about how it is becoming harder to breathe in some of the world's largest cities because of pollution caused to a large extent by automobile and factory emissions. How does that fit in?"

"You know, I asked essentially the same question of my finance professor after you had that incident with second-hand smoke at the coffee shop a couple of weeks ago. He said that dealing with those kind of environmental and social issues was the job of the government because companies couldn't know how much to spend or on what. I suppose he was correct when he said that decisions like that should reflect the judgment of all of society, not just a few firms."

"But isn't the argument of the invisible hand that the collective actions of individual businesses do reflect the judgment of society, at least in terms of the products and services people want to buy? Why can't the invisible hand incorporate these other issues as well? After all, I would think that saving the environment and achieving social justice should be just as important to society as economic well being."

"I suppose the argument is that companies get good signals about what to produce and sell from customers through the prices they're willing to pay for their products," replied Andrew thoughtfully. "But they don't get the same signals from customers about the environment or social justice."

"Sure they do," countered Jennifer. "Look at how the public responded to Three Mile Island, for example, and to those athletic shoe manufacturers that used child labor. It seems to me that those were pretty strong signals, and the companies responded."

"But those were one-time events, major incidents that were front-page news," Andrew objected. "Of course companies responded. They were thrust into the spotlight and had to. What I meant was that on a day-to-day basis companies don't get good information from customers."

"If they don't it's because the problem is the other way around," Jennifer replied. "It's the customers who don't get good information from companies." She picked up a metal tin of cookies from the coffee table and opened it to reveal the plastic form containing the cookies inside. "How much do we know about how this was made? How much energy was used to produce it and get it to the supermarket where we bought it? How much waste and pollution was there? Was everyone involved treated fairly? Will it all be reused when we are done with it or merely go into some landfill? The truth is that we don't know. Customers are already starting to demand that the companies they buy from act more responsibly. If customers got better information about the products and services they buy, companies would get better signals from their customers and could make better decisions about how they produce and sell."

"As for the government," Jennifer continued, "it doesn't seem like they do a particularly good job of setting some of society's boundaries. Look at how long it took them to raise fuel economy standards, and still not to a level that is going to make a real difference in reducing pollution.

It seems to me that what the government does too often reflects the political needs and philosophy of the party in power more than the needs of society. And what about all the lobbyists? Companies pay millions of dollars every year to influence the Congress not to pass legislation that would be costly to them, no matter how beneficial it would be for society. It's rare that the government steps in and acts against these interests. I think that if any change is going to happen, it is going to have to come from companies themselves."

Andrew listened carefully. Jennifer was not an expert in business or finance, but she was smart, and what she was saying made a lot of sense. Who was right about what was best for society? His professor, who argued that companies should be left alone to pursue the traditional goal of shareholder wealth maximization? Or, his fiancée, who was convinced that companies also had to include protecting the environment and pursuing social justice in their goals?

16

Trust

The air was no fresher on the other side of the door because the door did not lead to the street. Rather, Adam Smith found himself in a room that was as full of smoke as the one he had just left. However, the smoke in this room was primarily coming from fine cigars, not cigarettes, and had a distinctly different aroma. The decor of the room reminded Smith of the private clubs at Oxford, where the wealthier students met to eat, drink, and socialize. Smith was in Washington, D.C. The year was 1902.

Dark wood paneling was everywhere, and a large crystal chandelier hung from the ceiling in the center of the room. The walls were lined with bookshelves that were neatly filled with leather-bound books. A thick carpet covered the floor, and the room was furnished with several groupings of couches and armchairs, each covered in leather dyed a deep mahogany to match the wood paneling of the walls. There were five or six writing desks spread around the room with stationery, pens and inkwells, and a copy of the day's newspaper on each. If this building were a private club, then this room was most certainly its library.

Smith walked over to the nearest writing desk and picked up a piece of stationary and the newspaper. The engraved words at the top of the stationery informed him that this was indeed a private club and that it was located in Washington, D.C. The newspaper masthead also said 'Washington, D.C.' and was dated 1902. 'More than 125 years into the future,' Smith thought. He wished there were some way for him to learn what had happened politically and geographically in that time. 'Was this city named after the American general who was leading the rebellion against England? What country was abbreviated D.C., and where in the world was it located?'

Smith surveyed the library. There were men sitting alone, some reading the newspaper, others a book, and white-jacketed butlers were quietly circulating with drinks and cigars. His attention was drawn to one corner of the room where three men had pulled their chairs close together around a small coffee table and were deep in hushed conversation. They paused for a moment as a butler arrived and deposited three fresh glasses of Scotch whiskey on the table. As soon as the butler departed, the conversation resumed. Smith walked over so he could hear what was being said.

"Tell me again how you did it, John," asked the largest of the three men. "I always like hearing the story." He sat back and took a sip of his drink.

John D. Rockefeller replied. "It was very straight-forward, Pierpont. I was buying up as much of the competition as had been offered to me, but several large competitors remained."

"From what I've heard," said the third man, "you had been buying more than simply what had been offered to you. Take the 'Cleveland Conquest of 1872' for example. Isn't that what the press calls it? I find it hard to believe that such success was simply the result of casual negotiations."

"It certainly was not," interjected J. Pierpont Morgan. "Acquiring 22 of 26 competitors in less than two months requires a ruthlessness that few men possess. John made it clear to his competitors that if they didn't sell out to him, he would undercut their prices until they went out of business. It is no accident that he is now the world's richest man."

"Merely the result of my superior negotiating skills," said Rockefeller with a smile. He resumed his story. "As I was saying, there were some competitors that did not succumb to my powers of persuasion. These companies were, for the most part, well run and did not fear my putting them out of business as had the others before them. A new kind of 'arrangement' was needed. I was also facing the problem that every state has its own corporation law, often making day-to-day business unwieldy. So I had my lawyers create a new kind of organization: a trust to which we transferred the shares of each of my corporations. Now, one entity operates all of Standard Oil. With the increased efficiencies that resulted, I was able to 'convince' my remaining competitors to join the trust, to exchange their shares for certificates that would pay them dividends—and handsome dividends at that I might add. Together, we are able to be so much more powerful than remaining as competitors."

Turning to the third man present, Rockefeller asked, "Buck, how did you take control of the tobacco industry?"

"Initially, the same way as you did," James Buchanan Duke replied. "Recall that in 1885, I purchased the first license in the United States to use the newly-invented automated cigarette rolling machine. That immediately gave me control of nearly half of the domestic market as my major competitors couldn't match me for volume, consistency of product, or costs. They eventually sold out to me rather than go bankrupt, and the combination became the American Tobacco Company."

"Two of a kind!" chuckled J. Pierpont Morgan, his deformed nose turning even brighter purple and his huge frame bouncing on the chair in delight.

Duke smiled and continued. "More recently, my situation was a bit different than yours in that my primary remaining competition was from foreign companies, mostly British. So, we entered into an 'arrangement' to use your word, to divide the world market among us. American Tobacco now has exclusive rights to the United States, the Brits have exclusive rights to England and its territories, and we formed British-American Tobacco Company to jointly market to the rest of the world."

"Brilliant!" exclaimed Rockefeller. He turned to Morgan. "And now, with your purchase of U.S. Steel from Andrew Carnegie you join us as a 'captain of industry.' How are you going about consolidating your position?"

Morgan's face showed a slight degree of annoyance. "My good friend John, I would like to think that as a banker of my stature, I have been among your number for quite a while now."

Rockefeller replied quickly. "Of course, of course, Pierpont. Nobody can doubt the immensity of your role in the growth and consolidation of business for the last decades. My goodness, if not for your refinancing the national debt in 1895, this country that we love so much might well be bankrupt today. And as for your stature . . ."

The three men laughed heartily together as they realized Rockefeller was now referring to Morgan's ample size.

"But please continue Pierpont," requested Duke. "Tell us how you are ensuring that your markets will be yours and yours alone."

"My approach is to acquire companies in the industries that use steel—shipbuilding, railroads, bridge building, and so on. Then I can be certain that these companies will buy their metals only from U.S. Steel and not even consider a competitor's offer. Already, I have over 60% of the steel market."

Adam Smith thought about what he had just heard. These three men, in the pursuit of profits, had engineered massive consolidation in three of the most important industries of the day. In doing so, they had created what were essentially monopolies, and they now had the power to charge their customers any price the market would bear. Smith recalled a particular sentence from *The Wealth of Nations*:

> People of the same trade seldom meet
> together, even for merriment and diversion, but
> the conversation ends in a conspiracy against the
> public, or in some contrivance to raise prices.

His fears were being realized. This was certainly not a benefit for society. Smith took one more look at the sumptuous surroundings, then he turned and left the room through the same door by which he had entered.

17

Sharing the Wealth

Andrew closed the apartment door behind him and dropped his books on the dining table. Seeing Jennifer sitting at the computer on the other side of the living room, he walked over and gave her a kiss on the back of the neck. When her response was only to murmur "hello" without turning around, he asked, "What's up?"

"You've got me thinking, that's what's up."

"About what?"

Jennifer swung around on the chair. "About some of the remaining inequities in the world. You know that lately I've become interested in social history," she said, gesturing to several books on the coffee table. "One feature of recent history in most countries is a movement towards greater equality—equal rights, equal treatment, ability to vote, that kind of thing. Right now, I'm reading about income inequality." She turned back to the computer screen. "Did you know that nearly half of the world's population lives in poverty and more than 95% live on less than $10 a day?"

Andrew nodded. "I think that's one of those truths about the world that most well-off people try not to think about. It's such a huge problem. My guess is that people feel there's not much they can do to change things."

Jennifer turned back to the computer and called up a news article. "And listen to this. According to a major economic research organization, the richest 1% of all households own 35% of the world's wealth. It's even more concentrated at the top. One fifth of the world's wealth is owned by just the top 0.001%. How can that happen?"

"It sounds like you've been doing a lot of thinking independent of me. So how have I got you thinking?"

"You've been talking a lot about the relationship of business to some of the world's problems. I think this is more of the same. The way businesses operate is the source of much of these disparities."

Andrew thought for a moment. "Well, not everyone is equal when it comes to skills and abilities and the effort they put in. Some people deserve to be paid more, simply because they contribute more. I guess it's like a professional athlete or rock star, who can entertain thousands of people at a time. Don't they deserve to be paid very well given how much pleasure they give to so many people?"

"I suppose," said Jennifer. "But that doesn't account for the kind of income disparity I'm talking about. Most of the richest people in the world aren't athletes or entertainers. They're successful businessmen, or their descendants. And what about those billions of people in poverty? I can't believe they are at the bottom because none of them have anything to contribute."

"What's wrong with successful businessmen?" asked Andrew with mock indignation. "Seriously though, the opportunity to make a lot of money and become rich is an important factor that motivates people to invent new products and start new businesses. It keeps our economy vibrant. Look at how stagnant the economies of Eastern Europe were under the Soviet system when that motivation was taken away."

"I'm OK with that," Jennifer replied. "I have no problem if people who contribute a lot to others' well being and happiness earn good money. My concern is different. In fact, I have two concerns. One is that the difference in income between the rich and the poor is so great, even within one country."

"Some of that has to do with the cost of living," Andrew protested. "It costs a lot more to feed a family in some places than others. Some of those comparisons aren't totally fair."

"Sure, but that's relatively small stuff. How about the difference in pay between corporate executives and the rank and file?" Jennifer turned back to the computer and worked the keyboard for a minute. "Here's an article on executive pay. Look at the size of the bonuses some of these executives received last year. How can they justify enormous paychecks like that? That money came out of the pocket of every one of the company's stakeholders. In fact, if as you say, the goal of the firm is to maximize the shareholders' value, isn't this an example of managers doing exactly the opposite? Aren't they just taking a huge amount of money for themselves that should go to the shareholders? For me, that's not only bad business, it's a moral issue."

"I think you're right that some executives take too much money from their companies," agreed Andrew. He talked for a few minutes about the agency problem he had learned about in his finance class. "But top managers deserve to be paid well. Look at all the value they add for investors, the jobs they create, the money that gets pumped into the local economy. It's like those top athletes and entertainers."

"I don't think so," objected Jennifer. "You are making three assumptions I don't agree with. One is that these top managers make that much of a difference to the company's profitability. I'm sure some do, but . . ." She turned back to the computer. "According to this, there doesn't seem to be much of a correlation between executive pay and company performance. Performance goes up and down but pay stays high. Second, I don't believe that excellent managers are as rare as top athletes. Look, you are studying for your MBA to gain the skills to be an excellent manager. But so are tens of thousands of other young people every year. An awful lot of them are bright and highly motivated, just like you. I find it hard to believe that out of this huge pool of talent there are only a few that are really good. The other assumption I think is wrong is that only the best executives rise to the top. From what I've read, there are an awful lot of mediocre CEOs out there."

Andrew paused to digest the conversation. "You had a second concern about income distribution?"

"Yes. There are simply too many poor. Aside from the moral issue, there is a public security issue as well. Years ago, most of the world's poor were somewhat isolated and didn't know very much about the rich. But today, with information so widely available, these people know that they've gotten the short end of the stick. I don't think it's an accident that the rise of global terrorism came on the heels of the information explosion, or that many of the terrorists are recruited from the poor people of the world. What's that old Bob Dylan line from the 1960s, 'When you ain't got nothin' you got nothin' to lose!'? It seems to me that if more people had a stake in the global economy, the world would be a much safer place."

"What I really don't understand," continued Jennifer, "is why companies haven't gotten involved in these markets. There must be amazing opportunities to produce and sell all sorts of products and services to the poor. Sure, they don't have a lot of money now, but if companies got involved, they would create jobs which would pay incomes which would be spent on the companies' products and services. It would develop just like it has in the wealthier countries."

"I suppose," said Andrew, "although the governments of those poor countries would have to change. One reason that business hasn't developed in poor countries is that they don't have predictable political or legal systems. Companies don't want to invest money if they think they could lose it all overnight on the whim of some despot."

"Understood," replied Jennifer. "But how about here in our country. We have very stable political and legal systems, yet there are far too many poor people, and our country is not the only one like that. Also, remember our conversation about lobbyists? Businesses spend millions to influence our government to act in their interests. I can't believe they can't find a way to use some of that same influence to improve the stability of at least some poor countries. I just think businesses could do a whole heck of a lot more to alleviate poverty, if they decided it was the right thing to do. And I'm sure they could do it at a profit. They've missed a huge opportunity that would really help the world."

Jennifer paused for a moment. "You know, you talk a lot about the 'invisible hand.' It seems to me that the invisible hand operates only for people who are well off. If the invisible hand is so powerful, how come it seems to ignore more than half of the world's population? Or, maybe there are two invisible hands: one that holds the door open to prosperity for the well-off so they do better every year and another that holds the door shut for the poor and impoverished!"

18

The Protestant Ethic

On the other side of the door was a room that was as spartan as the previous one had been opulent. It appeared to be the work space for several people—there were six desks lined up two-by-three, and a seventh desk in the middle of the long wall facing the other six. Stacks of paper were everywhere, and other papers were tacked onto the walls at seemingly random intervals. Adam Smith walked over to the windows on the far wall. It was a bright, sunny day outside. Across the narrow street was a row of half-timbered buildings, and he could see a gently-flowing river a short distance away through the gaps between them. Smith was in Heidelberg, Germany. The year was 1905.

A man with dark hair and a closely cropped beard was sitting at one of the desks, reading a manuscript. As Smith turned away from the windows, two other men entered the room and drew up chairs to sit around the desk occupied by the bearded man.

"I believe we have now turned the corner," said one of the new arrivals who sported a bushy goatee and a pince-nez. "The numbers I have just received from our printer show that our circulation has doubled in the past six months."

His companion concurred. "Yes, and we are receiving many more submissions of scholarly articles."

"A remarkable achievement," said the seated man with a mischievous grin. He looked up at the other two. "Did either of my esteemed colleagues have any doubt that we would achieve the goals we set for our journal?"

"None whatsoever, Max," replied the man who had spoken first. "However, we must recall that it is less than two years since Edgar . . ." He nodded toward the third man. ". . . purchased the journal and we changed the name and editorial policy."

"Indeed," added Edgar Jaffé. "Given our focus, it seemed so much more appropriate to call the journal the *Archives for Social Science and Social Welfare.*"

"Yes," agreed Werner Sombart, adjusting the pince-nez on his nose. "But let us not forget that the success of the journal is due primarily to its content, and no article has been so widely read and discussed as the first part of Max's essay, 'The Protestant Ethic and the Spirit of Capitalism.'

I cannot wait until Max completes the second part of his essay so we can publish that as well. I'd wager that our circulation will double again."

Max Weber grinned broadly. "You flatter me, my friend. However, you shall not have to wait much longer as the essay is nearly completed. It requires only a few more strokes of the pen, and it shall be yours."

The excitement on the faces of Jaffé and Sombart was palpable. "Please, tell us all about it," Jaffé implored.

"You will remember that I commenced the essay by exploring how capitalism developed," Weber began. "The Industrial Revolution was far more than just the establishment of businesses based on the new technology of steam power. It was the birth of an entirely new economic system. Capitalism was unlike anything that preceded it. Why was it accepted? How did it take hold?"

"Clearly, one reason was the work of Adam Smith. He wrote about how these many new companies would create a benefit for society, even though each, somewhat selfishly, pursued its own interests. Smith made capitalism politically acceptable. But there is much more to the story. Society had to adapt to capitalism. Society had to accept that the individual pursuit of economic gain was correct. It is this social attitude I called the 'spirit of capitalism.'"

"So, the question then arises, what is the source of the spirit of capitalism? My thesis is that the foundations of capitalism can be traced to the Reformation. The origin of the spirit of capitalism is in the Protestant religions. It is not that these religions preached the tenets of capitalism. Rather it is that they encouraged rationality and hard work, sacrifice and thrift."

"Compare Protestant doctrine to that of Roman Catholicism. The Catholic Church provides its believers with access to the afterlife. Accept the church and its doctrines, and you shall be rewarded by salvation in heaven. However, there is no equivalent promise made to Protestants. Calvin, for example taught a doctrine of predestination, that at their birth God chose some people for salvation and others for damnation. So what was a Calvinist to do? How was he to know if he had been chosen for heaven or for hell? To keep his sanity, he had to develop a deep belief in the former. Self-confidence was required; self-doubt was a sign of insufficient faith. Only the most self-confident could be assured of a heavenly eternal life."

"But how could one know that he was sufficiently self-confident? The answer was that the people who were the most successful in their secular activities must be those with the most self-confidence. So, secular success, in particular the accumulation of wealth, became the route to divine salvation."

"Now, what could people do with their wealth? They couldn't spend it on luxuries since that was a sin to the austere Protestants. Giving it to the poor was yet another sin, condoning begging and laziness. The Catholic answer was to donate it to the Church, but most Protestant orders rejected fancy and expensive buildings, art, and icons. The only thing available was to invest the money, to become capitalists. So, the spirit of capitalism developed from the ethic of hard work, frugality, and investment of the Protestants."

"Therefore, what you are saying is that Protestant beliefs are necessary for capitalism to thrive," summarized Sombart when Weber had finished.

"No, not quite," responded Weber. "Protestantism was one important factor that launched capitalism, maybe the most important factor. But society is getting more secular every day, yet capitalism marches on. No, I believe that the ethic introduced to the world by Protestantism—hard work, frugality, investment—has since detached itself from its religious roots. One no longer needs religion to accept these values. On the one hand, this means that capitalism will endure, independent of what happens to religion. On the other hand, I fear that as the spirit of capitalism continues to drift away from religion, people will change their fundamental allegiance from the service of God to the service of industry. What will that mean for the greater good of mankind?"

Adam Smith found Max Weber's thesis provocative. As a Scottish Protestant himself, he was quite familiar with the beliefs and values of the people of the Industrial Revolution. Yet, he had never before made the connection between the teachings of his faith and capitalism. He smiled at the thought that the Scottish churches had played so important a role in the emergence of modern industry. And he agreed with Weber's concern about the loss of capitalism's religious underpinnings.

Smith took one last look at the three men, and then let himself out of the room.

−19−

False Gods

Andrew entered the apartment, untied his tie, and dropped the papers he was carrying on the dining table. He was in the last term of his MBA program, and, like most of his fellow students, he was in the midst of the final round of job interviews.

"You're home late," observed Jennifer. "Is that a good sign? How did it go?"

"Great," replied Andrew, plopping himself down on the couch. "And not so great."

Jennifer put down what she was doing and joined Andrew on the couch. Her look was one of concern. "What do you mean?"

"Well, they offered me the job . . . and I'm thinking seriously about turning it down."

"I don't understand. This is one of the companies you've been hoping to work for since before you went back to business school. All I've heard from you for the last two weeks is how excited you were to get called back for this interview. What happened?"

"Well, I did all the research we're advised to do before the interview. I read through the folders on the company at the university career office; I searched the Internet for news about the company and the industry; I even did an analysis of their most recent financial statements to be ready to talk about their strengths and weaknesses. I liked what I saw and was convinced that this was my first choice company, that I would grab an offer if they made me one."

"And . . .?"

"And I was very well prepared, just like I had hoped. I was able to talk intelligently about the company, and I had no trouble with the questions they asked me. But while I was sitting there, talking to some Vice President, I realized that while I knew an awful lot about the company's economic and financial condition, I knew very little about everything else."

"Like what?"

"Like the company's culture, for example, its attitudes, beliefs, values, that kind of thing. So, I asked if I could spend some time just wandering around the office, observing and talking to different people."

"And . . .?"

"And I wasn't so happy with what I found out. For one thing, I didn't get the sense that the company cared very much about the environment. One of the questions I asked was about how the company handled its recycling because I didn't see any bins designed to separate out different kinds of waste. It turns out I didn't see any because there weren't any. The company wasn't into recycling. Then, several people showed me a new electronic product they had developed. It was really cool, but a lot of the parts were plastic, and when I asked about whether the plastics were biodegradable they had no idea. And they had a lot of remaining inventory of the product this one replaced that would go straight to the dump."

"For another thing, there was a screen in the front of the office with the price of the company's stock in numbers large enough to be seen from everywhere in the room. It seems that management talks a lot about how employees should do something to increase the stock price every day. So I asked about how many employees participated in bonus plans tied to the stock price and found out that it was only top management."

"I guess the worst thing was that it didn't seem that the employees were all that happy to be there. Remember when I took my intro management course and learned about W. Edwards Deming, the guy who helped Japan get back on its feet after the Second World War?"

Jennifer nodded, although she honestly didn't remember.

"Well, Deming talked about 'joy in work,' the idea that people should be really excited to be at their jobs if they were to do their best work, and it was management's responsibility to create that culture. I just didn't see any of that."

"After I left the company, I needed some time to think, so I drove to school and went to the library to do more research on the company, especially on those environmental and cultural issues. That's why I was so late getting home."

"And did you find anything?"

"Nothing that changed my mind, and that's what's really bothering me now. I thought I knew what I was looking for. Now I wonder." Andrew's voice trailed off. He got a beer from the fridge and turned on the ball game. Jennifer went back to her work, knowing the best thing she could do was to give Andrew some space and time alone to think.

Later that night, as they lay next to each other in bed, it was clear that Andrew still was agitated. "Am I making the right decision?" he asked aloud, more of himself than of Jennifer.

She rolled onto her side and reached for his hand. "You have to make the decision that's right for you."

"I also have to make the decision that's right for us," Andrew replied. "If we're going to get married and have a family, I'm going to have to provide for us." Seeing the look on Jennifer's face, he quickly added, "Not that your income isn't critically important, but it's just that when we have kids, there will be a time when you most likely won't be working. And we both know that no matter how qualified you are, most women's salaries still aren't equal to what men make. Supporting the family will be primarily my job. How can I turn down this salary? How can I walk away from a career that will pay so well? What would I be doing to you and our future children?"

Jennifer moved closer to Andrew and hugged him. "When I said you have to make the decision that's right for you, I wasn't talking about money. We'll be OK. Really, we will. Whatever job you take will pay enough for us to live decently. Besides, you know I'm not in love with you for the cash. I love you for many reasons, and one of the most important is your character, what kind of person you are. I'd much rather we do what we think is really right than sell out for any amount of money, and I know you feel the same way. What's that phrase you use every so often? We have to 'walk the talk!'"

She kissed him on the forehead. "Deep down, do you feel that this is the wrong company to work for?"

"Other than the money, I really do."

"Then turning down their offer is the right decision for both of us," Jennifer said softly.

Andrew fell asleep that night in Jennifer's arms feeling better than he had for a long time.

20

Responsibility

Through the door Adam Smith found himself in a room lined with dark wooden bookshelves. Books of many colors occupied most of the shelves, but there were a substantial number of framed certificates and plaques on the shelves as well. Near the large windows on the far side of the room, a short, bald man with large eyeglasses and an effervescent personality was sitting behind a desk talking to several young men and women seated across from him. Smith was in Chicago, Illinois. The year was 1970.

Smith listened to the conversation for a few moments. The man behind the desk and his young visitors were engaged in a lively discussion. It did not take Smith long to realize that he was in the office of a professor at a university. He looked around the room again and concluded that this office would not be out of place at Oxford or at the University of Glasgow. In some ways, the universities of the future were just like the ones at which he had studied and taught. It was a comforting thought.

Smith walked over to the bookshelf on the wall to his left and looked at the books at eye level. Many had the word 'economics' in the title. Toward the left-hand side of the shelf was a copy of *The Wealth of Nations*. He smiled thinking about the number of people that must have followed him in exploring the subject that had excited him for the past ten years of his life.

One of the certificates caught his eye. It was from an academic society, acknowledging someone named Milton Friedman for service to the economics profession. He glanced at several of the other certificates and plaques. Each one congratulated Milton Friedman for one of his accomplishments. That must be the occupant of this office, thought Smith. That must be the man behind the desk.

Smith turned around and resumed paying attention to the conversation. One of the students was holding up a document. "I'm particularly interested in your essay of a couple of months ago, the one entitled 'The Social Responsibility of Business is to Increase Its Profits.' I don't understand how increasing profits can be the most socially responsible thing a business can do? Isn't social responsibility different from earning profits?"

Another student joined in. "And how about all the other things business can do to help society? I don't see why we shouldn't want businesses to do them as well?"

Milton Friedman smiled broadly. "This goes to the heart of the role of business in a free society. Let's take it one step at a time."

"First, the issue arises only in corporations where the managers of the business are not its owners. In other forms of business, where the owner and manager are the same person, there is no issue. If a proprietor wishes to spend money from his business on social issues, that's his prerogative in a free society."

"Now, in a corporation where the manager is not the owner, the manager's responsibility is to the people who do own the company, its shareholders. They've hired him for one purpose and one purpose only—to increase the value of their investment. If the manager spends corporate money on anything other than activities that increase profits, he is spending money that could otherwise be given to the shareholders. Of course, if they were given this money, they could choose to spend it themselves, and if they spent it in exactly the same way as the manager, there would be no problem. But this is rarely the case. Effectively the manager has taxed the company's shareholders and decided, without any process to inform him of shareholders' wishes, how to spend their money."

"Now, this raises two questions, one of principle and one of consequences. The question of principal is the same as that famous rallying cry of the American Revolution, 'taxation without representation.' If anyone is to impose taxes and spend the proceeds to further social goals, there should be a political system to ensure that the amount of the taxation and the direction of the spending are consistent with the desires of those who are taxed. No such system exists to serve as a check and balance on spending by corporate executives. Executives who spend on social causes are spending money in ways that the public has chosen not to. In this sense, what they are doing is profoundly undemocratic."

"And the question of consequences?" asked one of the students.

"That question is this: how can a corporate executive know the best way to spend money on social responsibility? How can he know what to spend it on? How can he know how much to spend? Surely he cannot know this, and thus there is no way to know if the consequences of his social spending are a benefit to society or not. Adam Smith saw this outcome 200 years ago when he wrote in *The Wealth of Nations*:

> **I have never known much good done by those**
> **who affected to trade for the public good."**

"Finally, businesses can't have responsibilities in the first place. Only people can have responsibilities. Businesses are simply the legal forms that surround the economic activities of people. So, to talk about the social responsibility of business makes no sense at all."

"My conclusion is simple." He picked up a copy of his best known book, *Capitalism and Freedom*, and searched for a particular page. "Here it is. 'There is one and only one social responsibility of business—to use its resources and engage in activities designed to increase its profits so long as it stays within the rules of the game, which is to say, engages in open and free competition without deception or fraud'."

Adam Smith turned away from the conversation and looked again at all the awards and honors on the bookshelves. Milton Friedman was certainly a highly regarded economist. His argument was cogent, and mostly consistent with what Smith believed and had written about in *The Wealth of Nations*. However, Smith saw two problems with it.

The first was that Friedman had quoted Smith to support his argument that businesspeople who attempt to contribute to the public good rarely succeed. But that was not what Smith had meant. That sentence was part of a discussion of the results of businessmen preferring to invest domestically rather than abroad. By doing so they helped the domestic economy grow faster than if they had invested elsewhere. Smith's point was an extension of the invisible hand. The alternative to businessmen making individual decisions about where to invest was some kind of organized campaign to persuade them to invest locally. As with production decisions, Smith doubted that such a campaign would lead to a better result than the combination of many individual decisions. He never meant to suggest that he was against businesses acting for the good of the public.

The second problem was philosophical. Friedman had argued that since businesses were not people they could not have responsibilities. Smith simply did not agree with that. As a former professor of moral philosophy, he well understood that businesses could not have the responsibilities that could only be attributed to people. But that did not mean that businesses had no responsibilities at all. He thought of the Latin phrase that had recently become a core value of the medical profession, *primum non nocere,* 'first do no harm.' It seemed to Smith that it would be irresponsible for a business knowingly to operate in a way that hurt people. Whether acting as individuals or within the structure of a business, everyone had a moral responsibility to live up to the accepted standards of society.

Adam Smith took one more look at the esteemed professor and his students, then turned around and left the office.

21

Copernicus

Through the door was a room in the shape of the letter L. On one side of the room were a couch, a plush chair, and some low tables. On the other side was a taller table surrounded by four straight-backed chairs, one of which was occupied by a young man who was working at the table. Adam Smith was in Jennifer and Andrew's apartment. The time was the present.

Andrew stared for a while at a piece of paper containing a diagram. Then he picked up a ballpoint pen and began sketching another diagram on a blank piece of paper. After about five minutes, he crumpled up his sketch, reached for another blank sheet, and began again. Smith looked around for an inkwell but couldn't find any. 'A pen that doesn't need ink? How is that possible?' he thought.

After another few minutes of sketching, Andrew shook his head. The answer wasn't coming easily. He got up and began pacing back and forth hoping the change of position would stimulate his thinking.

Just then the door to the apartment opened, and Smith watched as a young woman entered. She gave Andrew a look of amused curiosity. "What's up?" she asked, ". . . other than you."

Andrew grunted in frustration. "I've been working on this diagram all day now, but I can't seem to make any progress."

"Would it help if you talked it through with me?" offered Jennifer.

"It couldn't hurt. Do you have a few minutes?"

"Whatever you need."

Andrew picked up the paper with the diagram and showed it to Jennifer. Smith moved to where he too could see the paper and hear Andrew's explanation. "This is the first figure in Chapter 1 of my intro finance textbook. It's entitled 'Money flows of a business.' The company is represented by this picture in the center of the diagram. Surrounding it are the organizations that give money to it or receive money from it, or both. Over here are the company's suppliers and employees. This icon represents customers. Down here are the company's lenders and investors, and on this side are the government and the local community. The arrows show the flow of money between the parties."

"OK," said Jennifer. "So, what are you trying to do?"

"This diagram focuses only on money. That may have been all that mattered years ago, but today the relationship of a company to its stakeholders is much more complex than that. To take one example, if a company pollutes the air, it gives its stakeholders a lot more than money. It gives them impure air to breathe, and it contributes to climate change with all that that implies. I'm trying to redraw the diagram to take these other things into account."

"But beyond that, there is something else that bothers me about this diagram. When we took our first economics courses, we learned that economics was all about getting the maximum from scarce resources in order to produce the most for society." He looked at Jennifer's expression and smiled. "OK, I realize you may not remember that, but please bear with me. To the first economists, like Adam Smith, there were three types of resources used by companies: land, labor, and capital. Land and labor weren't particularly scarce. There was plenty of land on which to build factories and plenty of people willing to work in them. But capital—machinery and the money to purchase it—was comparatively scarce. So, in order to produce the greatest amount of goods and services for society, companies had to get the most they could from the money invested in them."

Adam Smith smiled. The conversation had turned to something he was quite familiar with.

Andrew continued. "Of course today, things are more complex than they were in the 18th century. Our concept of land has grown to encompass the minerals underneath it and the air above it, so today we call this 'natural resources.' And labor is no longer only blue collar. People are hired for their brains as well as their bodies, so now we call this resource 'human capital.' So, which one is the scarce resource today? Is it still financial capital? I'm not sure. I read all the time about how the world is awash with money looking for good investments. No, I'm convinced that for many companies, the scarce resource is people, especially for high-technology companies that need smart, well-educated, creative people to design and market their products. And given global warming and all the pollution that's taking place, it could be that for the world as a whole the scarce resource is natural resources, especially clean and abundant air and water."

"So," Andrew concluded, "should this diagram be only about money, or is that so last century? Come to think of it, the goal of the firm, maximizing the wealth of the shareholders, is based on the need to use financial capital efficiently. But if money is no longer always the scarce resource for companies, then the goal of the firm shouldn't always be about returns to investors. Maybe it should be about returns to scarce people skills, or even returns to the global environment." He sighed. "I wonder what Adam Smith would think if he were here today."

But of course, Adam Smith was there, standing just behind Andrew, and he was deep in thought. Smith had been wondering why he was in this particular flat with these two people. Now he understood. Andrew had just summarized many of the issues he had been learning about since his journey had begun. It was all coming together.

Jennifer studied the diagram and then looked up at Andrew. "You know what I think the problem is with this diagram? I think the problem is that the company is in the center with everything laid out around it. It almost looks like those old drawings of the universe with the Earth at the center from 1,000 years ago. I suppose that made sense back then when people saw the universe in simple terms. But as our knowledge grew, that scientist—what's his name—realized that the sun, not the Earth, was at the center of the planets, and even that wasn't the center of the universe."

"Copernicus," said Andrew. "His name was Copernicus." He thought for a moment stroking his chin. "You know, I really like that analogy. The current finance model was created over 200 years ago in a much simpler time. But now times have changed, and we have data about the environment and society that shows the limitations of that model. What we need is a new model of finance. We need a modern-day Copernicus!"

Jennifer went over to a bookshelf on the side of the room and brought back Andrew's copy of *The Wealth of Nations.* "Maybe you can find something in here that would help you."

Adam Smith looked at the book carefully. He thought he recognized a particular scratch in the leather cover. Was it . . . could it be . . . was this his own copy, the copy he kept on his desk in Kirkcaldy? He looked more closely. It *was* his own copy!

"You know," said Andrew, "I still find it amazing that you found this book in a country flea market. I keep trying to imagine how it got there, but I come up empty every time." He gave Jennifer a hug and went back to the dining table where he began a new diagram, this time with the Earth and all its living things at the center.

Adam Smith followed Andrew to the table and looked over his shoulder as he sketched. A feeling of deep frustration came over Smith knowing that Andrew could not see or hear him, that there was no way to have the conversation with Andrew that he was dying to have. How could he let Andrew know how much he agreed with him? He looked at his book which was now sitting on the dining table. Then he smiled.

Seconds later, Adam Smith walked to the front door and left the apartment.

22

False Dichotomy

Stepping through the door, Adam Smith found himself in a large room filled with circular tables. He counted twenty of them, each surrounded by eight chairs. Along one wall there was a platform with a speaker's podium in the middle and three chairs to either side. On the opposite wall was a long table with coffee, pastries, and fruit. A magnificent snow-capped mountain range was visible through the large windows that lined one side of the room. Smith was in Davos, Switzerland. The time was the present.

Behind the dais was a very large sign announcing that the day's activity was a conference with the title 'Profiting from Sustainability—How Economic Success, Environmental Success and Social Success Can Go Hand-in-Hand.' Groups of people were drifting into the room, helping themselves to breakfast, and finding seats at the tables. Smith took a seat at the back of the room.

At precisely 9am a man with round glasses and a mustache climbed onto the platform and went to the podium. He was followed by five other people who took the chairs to either side. "Good morning," the man began. The audience quieted down and turned to listen. "Welcome to the 'Profiting from Sustainability' conference. Many people believe that sustainability and profits are opposite sides of a coin, that it is impossible to have both at the same time. But as you will hear from our distinguished panel of speakers, if this ever was the case, it no longer is today. While it is certainly true that some approaches to sustainability can be costly, there are many ways to be sustainable and to contribute to sustainability that increase the bottom line." He introduced the others sitting on the platform, each of whom received a polite round of applause; then he took the remaining seat while another man stood and took his place at the podium.

The first speaker talked about the misconception that sustainability was always expensive. He pointed out that many acts like recycling waste cost very little and might even add to profits while contributing to sustainability. He talked about ways to reduce costs that were consistent with sustainability, such as eliminating unnecessary heating, cooling, and illumination. He gave examples of companies that had discovered that the by products of their own production processes could be reclaimed and used in other processes or sold at a profit as inputs to other businesses.

He concluded his talk by referring to the quality revolution of the 1980s and 1990s. "Back then, the widely-accepted belief was that quality was costly, that companies had to choose between low costs or high quality. Perhaps the clearest example was in the automobile industry where some luxury brands spent enormous amounts of money on quality control. That approach meant it was indeed expensive to produce high-quality cars. But then the Japanese manufacturers adopted systematic quality management methods and found they could produce high quality cars at a lower cost than before. For those companies, quality and profits were not opposites but went hand in hand. They did it by building quality into their designs, not by attempting to force quality into their products through after-the-fact inspections and rework. I am convinced the same is true of sustainability. Every day we are learning how to build sustainability into our products and production processes." He illustrated his remarks by talking about buildings that were being designed to require very little energy for heating and cooling yet cost virtually the same to construct as similar conventional buildings. "Soon it will be widely understood, just as we learned in the quality arena, that it is cheaper to be sustainable than not to be."

The next speaker talked about the development of new, environmentally friendly products. "The cost of these new products is declining daily. We're now to the point where, for many of them, it is becoming less costly to be sustainable than not to be. And customers are so excited about these products that even when they are not yet cheaper, they will pay a premium for them." He mentioned examples in heating and cooling, lighting, power generation, and engine design. "I forecast that very soon the market for products that are not environmentally friendly will simply dry up. Products will have to be sustainable to be acceptable."

The third speaker discussed the emerging markets for trading emissions credits. "These cap-and-trade markets put a price on carbon and other emissions which changes them from externalities to real costs. Companies that emit more than the target level of pollutants can only do so by buying credits from other market participants. On the other hand, companies that are able to reduce their emissions below target levels can sell unneeded credits and profit from their sustainability efforts." He talked about the success of the acid rain program in the United States and the mixed experience in implementing the 1997 Kyoto Protocol. He concluded his remarks by commenting on the development of voluntary markets, notably the Chicago Climate Exchange. "There is an exciting opportunity for companies that are committed to sustainability to profit by participating in these voluntary markets."

The fourth speaker spoke of the development of microfinance. "When we talk of sustainability, it is important to consider how the business organizations of the developed world can better serve the underdeveloped part of our planet. In the past, financial institutions ignored the poor. The risk of non-repayment, the lack of acceptable collateral, and the cost of managing many small accounts made this an unprofitable business. The result was that the poor paid excessively high fees and interest rates for loans and other financial services if they could get access to them at all. Today all that is changing." He described how financial institutions, some established and some newly created, were discovering new ways to serve the poor, by offering savings accounts, small loans, emergency funds, and assistance with major events such as weddings, childbirth, and education. "We have discovered how to turn serving the world's poor into a profitable business. It's a win-win situation."

The final speaker talked about the development of goods and services to meet the needs of people in developing markets. "The growth of these markets has been very similar to the growth of microfinance. Companies are learning how to package and market their products in ways that third-world customers can afford. One soap manufacturer, for example, has developed single use packages and, along with it, an education campaign to teach the benefits of cleanliness to people who have never used soap before. The company not only has created a profitable business, the increased soap usage is reducing the incidence of illness and disease. I can imagine many opportunities like this to serve the less fortunate in a profitable way."

When all the speakers had finished, the moderator returned to the podium. He thanked each speaker by name which elicited rounds of applause from the attendees. Then he summarized the morning. "What I hope you have heard and will take away from these presentations is that the ways that companies can contribute to the environment and the needs of society, and do so at a profit, are limited only by your imagination. The assertion that meeting environmental and social needs can not coexist with profits is simply not true. As you have heard today, there is plenty of evidence to the contrary, and the evidence is growing daily."

He continued. "I want to challenge every one of you to rethink how your company operates, and in particular, to rethink your company's goals. If all you do is focus on maximizing profits or shareholder wealth, you risk missing the greatest opportunities for growing your business that we have seen in a long time. Every company should be thinking about how to integrate these sustainability opportunities into their business model. One way to summarize this is through a phrase I'm sure many of you have heard before, the 'triple bottom line.' People, planet, profits. Each is important. Each contributes to the well being of the global community. All three can be achieved in harmony with each other."

"That concludes our morning program. After lunch we will reconvene for the discussion sessions. Each of our speakers will be in one of the breakout rooms across the hall. There is a sign posted outside each door indicating who will be in each room. Please go to whichever discussion most interests you or feel free to wander among the rooms. Thank you, and enjoy your lunch."

Adam Smith stood up and watched as the conference attendees slowly left the room. The speakers that morning had crystallized some thoughts he had been tossing around for some while now. Environmental sustainability and financial success were not mutually exclusive. Neither were social responsibility and financial success. It was possible to be profitable and simultaneously contribute to the health of the world. The opportunities were numerous and growing. The key was to move away from focusing solely on profit maximization. Companies that learned how to integrate the environmental, social, and financial would be the successful firms of the future.

By now the room was empty. Smith lingered for a while looking at the spectacular landscape outside the windows. Then he turned and left the room.

–23–

Transformation

Andrew held the elaborately-carved wooden door open for Jennifer and followed her inside. The second year of his program had flown by, and he had taken his last final examination that afternoon. In less than two weeks he would graduate with his MBA degree. To celebrate, Jennifer had made reservations at the best restaurant in town.

The maitre d' sat them at a candlelit table in the corner and expertly unfolded their napkins and placed them on their laps. "Better service than I get at home!" said Andrew with a big grin.

"Me too!" agreed Jennifer, her smile just as wide.

They chatted about Andrew's last exam while reading the menu. Then, the waiter took their food order, and the wine steward suggested an excellent Bordeaux to compliment their selections.

When the wine arrived, and Andrew had completed the obligatory smelling of the cork, sipping the first pour, and complimenting the selection, Jennifer raised her glass. Andrew followed her lead. "To the future!" she toasted.

"To the future!" Andrew repeated. "Our future. And to how important your love and support have been to me these past two years."

Jennifer smiled modestly. "I did very little. This is all your accomplishment."

"You did much more than you may think," Andrew replied. "When I began the program, I thought I knew what I wanted from my career, you know, big company, big office, big money." He smiled. "You changed all that."

"Should I apologize?" asked Jennifer with a twinkle in her eyes.

"Far from it. You helped me get past my fixation on earning a big salary. You helped me see what was really important to me." He paused. "I guess what I'm saying is that you helped me become a much better person."

"You were a very good person when I met you," said Jennifer. "I didn't fall in love with you hoping to turn you into someone else. But you have changed over these past two years." She thought for a moment. "A better way to say it is that you've grown as a person." She smiled. "Isn't that what education is supposed to do?"

"This experience certainly did change me," agreed Andrew. "It opened my eyes to alternatives I never would have thought of before going back to school, and it really helped me clarify my values."

"I think the biggest thing that I saw is that you got so into sustainability. Two years ago if you thought at all about environmental or social issues, it was only in passing. Now you are passionate about them."

"No question," Andrew agreed. "But it's much more than that. When I started my program, I couldn't see much connection between business and sustainability, and I certainly didn't see any connection between finance and sustainability. My finance professors never even talked about sustainability. They taught us how to make money, how to add financial value to a company. After all, that is what they said was the goal of the firm. But then I started asking them questions, to a large extent because you started asking me questions, and I began to realize the limitations of the existing theories. If I had to pick a point where my true business education began, that would be it."

"I never told you this, but there was a point about half-way through the program when I was almost ready to quit. I was so upset about how much of global warming was caused by business activities and how businesses weren't addressing urgent social problems, that I questioned whether it was the right place for me. I really got scared that I might get caught up in the life style or seduced by the money and become part of the problem. But then I realized that if change was going to take place, much of it, maybe most of it, was going to have to come from business itself. Business has to be the leader in creating a better world, just as it has been for the past 200 years in the economic arena—jobs, food, clothing, shelter. The opportunities for business to make a difference are huge, and I want to be a part of it."

They ate without speaking for a while, each thinking about how they complimented each other and how they were continuing to grow together as a couple. Andrew broke the silence. "To the future!" he said softly. "Wasn't that your toast when I began my program nearly two years ago?"

Jennifer smiled and nodded.

"Maybe your toast was more prescient that either one of us could have known back then. Maybe we are toasting much more than my future or our future tonight. Maybe we are toasting the future world that we will leave to our children. Maybe we are toasting what we and others like us can do to make the world a better place."

Jennifer reached across the table and placed her hand on his. Andrew smiled, then laughed softly.

"What's funny?" asked Jennifer.

"I'm thinking about that conversation we have every time we eat at our favorite café," he replied. "You know, the one where I wonder why I read the menu since it never changes"

Jennifer nodded.

"Well, your standard reply is that the day I stop reading it is the day it will change. I just wonder if that applies to finance theory as well."

"What do you mean?"

"I wonder if one reason finance continues to argue for shareholder wealth maximization is that so many people— students, professors, finance executives—are reading the same menu of finance theory over and over. Maybe it's time to stop reading that menu for a while so the creative finance chefs among us can update it."

As they drove home, they talked about 'walking the talk,' about what they both could do personally to become more sustainable in their lives. They discussed ways they could become more aggressive in recycling their trash and other waste. They commented on the large vehicles they passed and vowed to purchase energy efficient cars in the future. They discussed how they could further reduce their energy use at home and lower their carbon footprint.

When they arrived at the apartment, Jennifer went into the bedroom and Andrew sat down on the couch. There was so much swirling through his mind—the exhilaration of finishing his degree, his love for and future with Jennifer, how much he was anticipating a job interview later in the week with a company that had a growing reputation for sustainability. He turned on the ball game and went to the kitchen to get something to drink. As he returned to the couch, he noticed his copy of *The Wealth of Nations* in the adjacent bookshelf. 'So, this is where it all started,' he thought. He pulled the book from the shelf, and as he did so, several pieces of paper fell out onto the floor. He frowned and looked at them carefully. Judging from their color, they were as old as the book. Carefully, so as not to tear them, he unfolded them and spread them out on the coffee table. While the ink had faded somewhat, the words were still clear and readable. It was a letter, and it was signed by Adam Smith himself. Slowly, Andrew read the letter. Then, in disbelief, he read it again.

"Jenny!" he shouted. "Jenny, where are you? You've got to see this!"

Jennifer quickly came into the room, not sure whether to be excited or concerned. "What is it?"

"Look at this," said Andrew, directing her attention to the papers.

"What is it?"

"I think it's a letter written by Adam Smith. It just fell out of the book," he said pointing to *The Wealth of Nations* on the table next to the papers. He read the letter out loud to Jennifer. "This is exactly what we have been talking about." Then he frowned. "But how could Adam Smith have known that global sustainability would become a crucial issue more than 200 years after he wrote *The Wealth of Nations?*" He stopped and looked up questioningly at Jennifer.

Jennifer studied the letter once more. "The amazing thing to me is that of all the people who might have discovered Smith's letter, it was you, someone who is about to devote his personal life and professional career to sustainability."

Andrew sat back on the couch. He exhaled slowly. "Yeah, it is amazing. Really amazing. It's almost as if Adam Smith wanted to talk directly to me!"

—— *The Letter* ——

Adam Smith stared out the window at the lawn outside his house. It was a beautiful day, but he saw none of it. He was too busy thinking about all he had learned. He turned around, crossed the room, and sat down at his desk. He opened his copy of *The Wealth of Nations* and reread the paragraphs leading up to the 'invisible hand.'

Smith thought long and hard about the last sentences. Was profit maximization wrong? Not today in 1776, he concluded, but it will be in the future. He recalled the businesses he had written about in *The Wealth of Nations*, small and without any economic, social, or political power. These businesses had a tiny effect on the environment and even less on society, if they had any effect at all. The only area they could influence was economic. Profit maximization did an excellent job of motivating these businesses to create wealth, the basis of economic success. Instructing these businesses to maximize profits indeed led them to do the best they could for society.

But Smith now knew that the businesses of the 21st century would be different, much more numerous and much larger in size and influence. They would have the power to impact the environment and society. Instructing them to maximize profits would lead them to excel in the economic arena, but at the expense of the environmental and social. Yet, all three were aspects of sustainability. All three were needed by society. Any one without the others was insufficient. A new goal for business was required, one that embraced the economic benefits that derived from profit maximization, but went further to address environmental and social sustainability goals.

Smith took out a piece of paper and dipped his pen into the inkwell. Then with the same clear hand he had used when writing *The Wealth of Nations*, he set down his conclusions.

> In 'An Inquiry Into the Nature and Causes of the Wealth of Nations' I described how the decisions of business owners, although intended to enrich only themselves, yield a benefit for society due to the actions of the markets for the products they produce, the 'invisible hand.'
>
> The societal benefit to which I was referring was that of using the scarce

resources of the world in the most efficient manner. Since land and labor were relatively abundant, the scarce resource was capital. It was this resource that had to be used wisely, and the way to do that was for each business to maximize its profits. By doing this, they became efficient producers and yielded the highest possible returns to the capital they employed. Capital flowed to the most efficient businesses; hence the scarce resource was deployed in the most efficient manner.

In the future, this fundamental principle of economics will remain true. It will be equally as important then as it is today to use scarce resources wisely so as to produce the maximum benefit for society. However, in the future the scarcest of resources will not always be capital. Natural resources, today simply land, and human resources, today simply labor, will each be the scarce resource at some times and in some places. Maximizing the returns to capital will not always create the maximum benefit for society.

Today businesses are small and do not have the ability to affect, in any significant way, the quality of the environment or the fabric of society. Even though it is possible that in the act of maximizing profits, businesses might damage the environment or hurt society, such impairment is insignificant and can be safely ignored in comparison to the great benefits businesses are creating in the economic realm.

I now know this will not always be the case. Businesses will grow in size and complexity. The largest will employ many thousands of people and will operate both domestically and internationally. Their impact on the world will be significant. They will have the capacity to do immense damage to the environment and society.

Some observers will claim that the economic benefits of businesses are so great that nothing should be done to constrain them. They will argue that businesses should be left alone to continue to create wealth, regardless of any damage they might cause to the environment and to society. However, I now know that in the future this damage will occur and will threaten the very existence of man. It will be impossible to ignore.

Others will claim that it is the role of governments to constrain business and in this way prevent the damage. This is insufficient. Governments everywhere will remain influenced by the wealthy and by businesses themselves. They will be all too slow to respond and then only to damage so egregious that it leads to public outcry. When they do respond, it will be after much of the damage is done.

The solution must lie within business itself. Such will be the power of the businesses of the future that their goal can no longer solely be financial if society wishes to derive from them the maximum benefit. Rather, they must find a balance among the need to serve society in the realms of economics, the environment, and social order. I am convinced that it will be possible to find this balance, a new goal for business that will continue to yield high profits while at the same time serving the other needs of society

The world is constantly undergoing change. Theories that were valid in one era rarely hold up in the long run. At the minimum, they must evolve. In some cases they must be discarded completely to be replaced by newer ones that better explain and predict and can be used to guide behavior. It is folly to cling to a theory that has clearly outlived its usefulness. In the same way, the institutions of society must retain sufficient flexibility to adjust when it is clear that they are restraining change. There is too much evidence throughout history of institutions that placed far too much faith in existing theories, and in doing so prevented change and set back the development of the world by centuries.

I retain the utmost faith in the invisible hand. The combined decisions of the many will still produce better results than those of the few. The power of markets to direct resources will remain one of the true wonders of human interaction. If the businesses of the future listen carefully, the markets will guide them to what they must do to best serve mankind, to remain *the great economic benefactors of the world while simultaneously creating a better environment and a better society for all humanity.*

Adam Smith
Kirkcaldy, 1776

Adam Smith stood up, leaned over his desk, and reread the letter as the ink dried. He paused as he reached the last paragraph:

I retain the utmost faith in the invisible hand...

The invisible hand! A curious look came over his face. Was there a hint of a smile?

There was just one more thing he had to do. Carefully, Smith folded the letter and tucked it into the back of his own copy of *The Wealth of Nations*. Then, putting the book under his arm, he crossed to the other side of his study, took a deep breath, and opened the door to the parlour.

It was as he had hoped. Stepping through the door, Smith found himself on the edge of a large lawn on a bright summer day. The lawn was filled with tables. Beside each one was a vendor exhibiting his wares. Smith quickly found the one he was looking for, a bookseller. Jennifer was standing next to the table looking at the books. Was he in time? She looked away, and at that moment Smith put his copy of *The Wealth of Nations* on top of several books toward the back of the table. He held his breath. Then, she turned back toward the table and picked up his book.

Adam Smith stayed long enough to see Jennifer purchase the book. Then, knowing that his journey had come to an end, he let out a sigh of relief, went over to a shop on the edge of the field, and walked through the door.

References and Notes

1 – The Invisible Hand

Quotations from: Smith, Adam, *The Wealth of Nations*, Book IV, Chapter 2; Smith, Adam, *The Theory of Moral Sentiments*, Part IV, Chapter 1.

It is believed by some scholars that Adam Smith dictated *The Wealth of Nations*, rather than wrote it by hand as in this book as his penmanship was poor and he claimed to dislike writing.

4 – Truth

Adam Smith makes numerous references to the politics and economics of Britain's American colonies in *The Wealth of Nations*, Books IV and V.

Descriptions of the lecture taken and Al Gore's statements paraphrased or quoted from *An Inconvenient Truth*, Lawrence Bender Productions, 2006.

6 – Inconvenient

Descriptions of the lecture taken and Al Gore's statements paraphrased or quoted from *An Inconvenient Truth*, Lawrence Bender Productions, 2006.

Quotations from: Smith, Adam, *The Wealth of Nations*, Book I.

8 – Sustainability

Information about the United Nations Environment Programme is available from the UNEP web site: http://www.unep.org/.

Quotation from: *Our Common Future, Report of the United Nations World Commission on Environment and Development*, New York, United Nations, 1987.

Information about the United Nations Global Compact is from the UN Global Compact website: http://www.unglobalcompact.org/.

Information about the United Nations Environment Programme–Finance Initiative is from the UNEP-FI website: http://www.unepfi.org/.

10 – Suboptimization

Quotation from: Smith, Adam, *The Theory of Moral Sentiments*, Part IV, Chapter 1.

11 – Agency

The term stakeholder has been defined in several ways. Other definitions include "a party who affects, or can be affected by, the company's actions" (Freeman, R. Edward, *Strategic Management: A Stakeholder Approach*. Boston: Pitman, 1984), and ". . . individuals and constituencies that contribute, either voluntarily or involuntarily, to [a corporation's] wealth-creating capacity and activities, and . . . are therefore its potential beneficiaries and/or risk bearers." (Post, James E, Lee E. Preston, and Sybille Sachs, *Redefining the Corporation: Stakeholder Management and Organizational Wealth*. Stanford, CA, Stanford University Press, 2002).

The professor's data on stock ownership in 2005 is from: Investment Company Institute and the Securities Industry Association, "Equity Ownership in America, 2005." 2005, New York and Washington D.C.

14 – *Communism*

Quotations from: Smith, Adam, *The Wealth of Nations*, Book I.

16 – *Trust*

Quotation from: Smith, Adam, *The Wealth of Nations*, Book I.

17 – *Sharing the Wealth*

Jennifer's data from: World Bank Development Indicators 2008 as reported by Shah, Anup in "Poverty Facts and Stats," at http://www.globalissues.org, September 3, 2008; Boston Consulting Group global wealth report as reported by Giannone, Joseph A., "World's Richest Got Even Richer Last Year" Report, Reuters Limited, September 4, 2008.

Song lyric from: Dylan, Bob, "Like a Rolling Stone." Copyright 1965, renewed 1993, Special Rider Music.

20 – Responsibility

Milton Friedman's statements paraphrased from Friedman, Milton, "The Social Responsibility of Business is to Increase Its Profits." The New York Times Magazine, September 13, 1970.

21 – Copernicus

Figure "Money flows of a business" from Werner, Frank M. and James A.F. Stoner, *Modern Financial Managing— Continuity and Change*, 3rd edition, update 3.2. p. 4. 2010, Freeload Press, St. Paul, MN.

Credits

Fonts

Adam Smith's handwriting is set in Karine font created by Philippe Blondel. Obtained as freeware from www.fontspace.com.

Printed work from Adam Smith's books is set in JSL Ancient font created by Jeffrey S. Lee. Obtained as freeware from http://www.shipbrook.com/jeff/typograf.html.

Made in the USA
Middletown, DE
10 September 2021

47893807R00099